LUCKY EDDIE

*The Life, Times, and Family of
Former U. S. Congressman
Edward G. Breen*

by Edward Focke Breen

*with a preface by
the Honorable Tony P. Hall*

The Local History Company
publishers of history and heritage

Pittsburgh, Pennsylvania, USA

Published by   The Local History Company
112 North Woodland Road
Pittsburgh, PA 15232
www.TheLocalHistoryCompany.com
info@TheLocalHistoryCompany.com

The name "The Local History Company", "Publishers of History and Heritage", and its logo are trademarks of The Local History Company.

Library of Congress Cataloging-in-Publication Data

Breen, Edward Focke, 1957-
  Lucky Eddie : the life, times, and family of former U.S. congressman Edward G. Breen / by Edward Focke Breen ; with a preface by Tony P. Hall.
     p. cm.
  Includes bibliographical references and index.
  ISBN-13: 978-0-9770429-8-2 (trade pbk. : alk. paper)
  ISBN-10: 0-9770429-8-7 (trade pbk. : alk. paper)
  1. Breen, Edward G., 1908-1991. 2. Breen, Edward G., 1908-1991—Family. 3. Legislators—United States—Biography. 4. United States. Congress. House—Biography. 5. Mayors—Ohio—Dayton—Biography. 6. Hotelkeepers—United States—Biography. 7. World War, 1939-1945—Mediterranean Region. 8. World War, 1939-1945—Participation, American. 9. Dayton (Ohio)—Biography. I. Title.
  E748.B8414B74 2008
  328.73092—dc22
  [B]
                                          2008039964

Printed in USA   1.0

CONTENTS

Lucky Eddie

This book is dedicated to my wife Cathy, who makes my world bright and beautiful, and to my sons Jamie and Robert, who I hope will keep alive the stories of their ancestors. It is also dedicated to my mother and late father, whose lives form the core of this book, as well as to the memories of my Uncle Bob and Aunt MaryLouise Garrity who I miss very much. Their kindness and generosity made a difference in this world as well as to me personally. Finally, I would be remiss not to include my wonderful maternal grandparents, the late Elmer and Marie Focke, who taught me many things about life in the course of adding a few stories of their own.

Every night when I go to bed I ask myself: What did we do today that we can point to for generations to come, to say that we laid the foundation for a better and more peaceful and more prosperous world?

Lyndon B. Johnson,
President of the United States, in a speech given April 21, 1964

Whatever the challenge, he [Edward G. Breen] did his best, in good conscience, and for that we owe him.

Laurence Newman,
former associate editor and columnist for the Dayton Daily News, *1987*

PREFACE

Eddie Breen was a legendary figure in Ohio political life. My family knew the Breen clan well over the years, going back to the days when my grandfather was a business associate of John Breen's, Eddie's father and a celebrated hotel man in the early part of the twentieth century. I grew up hearing my own father's stories about Eddie, a man who lived life to the fullest. Eddie Breen always cared deeply about the people who worked for him in the hotel business and who served under him in the army. Later, that caring extended to those whom he served as mayor and congressman. I can personally attest to his popularity and the strong feelings his constituents had for him, as my father, Dave Hall, was constantly reminded when he became Dayton's mayor, and as I was later when I was elected to represent the same congressional district.

Growing up in the hotel business gave Eddie and his siblings a window on a sophisticated world and taught him how to move in it, as did the family good fortune that made it possible for him to travel and gain insights far beyond those typical of someone from a small Midwestern city in early-to mid-twentieth century. He was a genuine war hero who upon his return used his talents throughout the rest of his life to better his hometown.

The book is not a simple biography of a wonderful man, although his story is at its heart. Eddie's sister, the later MaryLouise Breen Garrity, for instance, is a distinguished character in her own right, and the author manages to overcome some of her life-long reticence to share details of her exploits, giving the reader a taste of this remarkable woman (among other things, she was a spy during World War II). As a family memoir, the book portrays a fascinating array of people in an America that no longer exists, chronicling their rise from poor immigrants to citizens solidly woven into the fabric of the nation. It is a story that we all should read and remember, as it reminds us what has made this country great.

The Honorable Tony P. Hall

United Nations Ambassador, former Congressman (D), Ohio Third Congressional District, and three-time Nobel Peace Prize Nominee

INTRODUCTION

*Katherine, MaryLouise and Edward G. (Eddie)
Breen on vacation in California, circa 1920.*

Storytelling has been a tradition in the Breen family for as long as I can remember. I always loved hearing the tales my father told, many of which he had heard from his father.

The nineteenth century was the great age of emigration to this country. My father's family followed that path (the Breens from Ireland and, on his mother's side, the Beckmans from Germany). They came not to the large eastern coastal cities, but to the Midwest, the Beckmans to Cleveland and the Breens to Dayton.

Edward G. Breen, my father, and John P. Breen, my grandfather, were hotelmen in an age when every city had its grand and elegant establishment—establishments the two operated and sometimes owned in Dayton, Ohio and other areas as far away as Chicago and Buffalo. They learned to use their natural Irish charm as hosts, befriending people they would otherwise never have known, while always remembering their immigrant roots.

My father was always very proud of his years as a hotel man. Many times I would be with him in his later years and someone would ask him what line of work he had been in. More than once, I jumped in to proudly say, "My father was in the motel business." My father would then correct me, "No, I was *never* in the motel business, I was in the *hotel* business." To him, there was a great distinction.

World War II thrust my father and his sister into situations where they met and became close to a fascinating array of people, many of whom remained lifelong friends. My father successfully entered politics, first as mayor of Dayton then as a United States Congressman, adding another entirely different layer of stories to the mix. It certainly never hurt that for years he was considered one of the most handsome and eligible bachelors at home and beyond until he married my mother—that alone guaranteed him more than his share of "ink" in the Midwestern media over time.

Remembering his Irish roots affected my father's behavior during his entire life. Like many of his era, he strongly believed in superstitions and good luck charms. In fact, as an adult he always carried a four leaf clover encased in plastic as his good luck charm. He also always made sure to spit between his fingers three times if he saw a black cat and, if that black cat walked across the road in front of him, he turned around and found another route. This aggravated me to no end when we were in the car driving somewhere and ended up late time and again. He also made sure never to walk under a ladder or look backwards into a mirror. I think he believed taking these precautions were what helped him survive the tragic Dayton flood as a child and helped enable him to keep a job during the Great Depression while others lost theirs, as well as surviving the horrors of World War II and coming home to Ohio to win every election he ever entered. It must have worked for him, because he was through all of his life, "Lucky Eddie."

*Eddie Breen, future United States Congressman
and Mayor of Dayton, Ohio, circa 1910.*

I might have been a skeptic about some of the family's more out-rageous claims, except for the amazing amount of documentation that exists—albums of photos, boxes of newspaper clippings, menus, campaign flyers, you name it. Family members were often in the news, resulting in a wealth of coverage.

I hope the reader will find an interesting glimpse into a style of life that no longer exists in the United States. Bear in mind, though, that these stories are told in the context of their time period and from my father's point of view. What I found compelling was a chance to understand the themes of our family as I have always heard them presented: how sharing stories enriches lives; the importance of racial and religious tolerance; the value of service; and the willingness to care when the need presents itself, not simply when it's convenient.

COMING TO AMERICA

Twelve men were listed in the 1892 Xenia, Ohio city directory as draymen; the cart shown in the front left of this photo, taken on April 19, 1891 is similar to Maurice Breen's. Courtesy of the Greene County Historical Society.

My family's long tradition of storytelling originated in Killarney, County Kerry, Ireland, where on chilly evenings, the early Breen ancestors probably huddled together before a warm fire. (The place name "Kilbrean More" in the Killarney area is derived from the Breen name and means "large woods of Breen".) My forefathers did not have books; even if they could read, which was highly unlikely, they would not have been able to afford them. Storytelling served multiple purposes at the time: passing down of family history, teaching of moral lessons, and providing entertainment. In so doing, the Irish instilled a

*Maurice Breen in the only known photo of him, probably
taken at the time of his son John's wedding in 1896.*

tradition that carried through the generations, even while the content
changed as the family eventually lifted itself out of poverty.

Coming to America was likely the only way out of a life of poverty
and prejudice for my great-grandfather, Maurice Breen, who left Ireland in the 1850s. Maurice, a tenant farmer, had known great hardship
and heartbreak in Ireland due to the harsh rules set against Catholics
by the ruling British Protestants, such as forbidding Catholics an education (Maurice never learned to read or write). After the potato crop
failed several years in a row, Maurice emigrated, joining his brothers
Daniel and Patrick, and sister, Catherine, who had left for the United
States a few years earlier. Maurice settled in Xenia, Ohio—a major railroad town with a large Irish population.

The Union Depot, Dayton, Ohio in 1890. John P. Breen is second from the right leaning his elbow on his neighbor's shoulder; he owned the restaurant at the depot for many years. The photo appeared in the Daily News *on December 26, 1943 courtesy of George W. Brunett.*

Once settled in the United States, Maurice went into the draying business, hauling logs and steel for the railroads. He met Mary O'Neal, another Irish immigrant, and they married in November 1851. As a poor Irish family, the Breens lived a life in America that could have existed only in their wildest dreams had they stayed in Ireland—poor as they were, in Ohio they had food, shelter and opportunities that they capitalized on within a generation. My grandfather, John P. Breen, was born in April of 1860. By the time John came along, he already had three older siblings (Mary, Catherine, and Daniel) and was quickly joined by four younger ones: Maurice, Jr., Hanna, Michael, and Frank.

After having personally experienced his own share of prejudice in Ireland, Maurice had little use for the racial prejudice that existed in America. He made it a matter of course to do business with all men and to treat them equally, instilling this trait in his children from a very early age. Maurice transported runaway slaves on the Underground Railroad by hiding them in his draying wagon amongst his load of steel train parts. Despite the danger, Maurice was assisted by his family and the Irish community who, recalling their servitude to the English, felt the risks taken for freedom were worth the price of discovery. In fact, so instilled was this attitude of equality within the family that Xenia's *Daily Gazette* noted years later in Maurice's nephew, Daniel E. Breen's June 18, 1897 obituary:

> . . . the expressions of sympathy seemed to come from all classes, for Dan's popularity was with black and white, rich and poor alike, and with the latter he will be especially missed, for his large heart knew no bounds with those whom he knew to be in need. . .

When Maurice died in 1906, the headline in the same Xenia paper and the following article told it all:

> QUAINT CHARACTER WAS MR. MORRIS [sic] BREEN -- The News of Whose Death at Marion, Ohio Was Received in Xenia on Tuesday Morning—The news was received in Xenia on Tuesday of the death in Marion, Ohio, of Mr. Morris Breen. For many years he was one of the best known citizens of this city, and while he had been absent from Xenia for two or three years past, there will be few who will not recall him and remember some quaint remark or joke, of which he always had an abundant fund. IIe was an Irishman through and through, good-hearted and possessed of a ready wit which was at once so quaint and so original that he never failed to provoke unbounded mirth wherever he appeared with one of his unexpected sallies of humor.
>
> He came to Xenia long ago, the greater part of his manhood being spent here. At first he was employed on the Pennsylvania railroad in the days when steam railroads were just beginning to be operated. He was a trackman for a time, and then he took up the business of draying. One of the most familiar sights in Xenia for a great many years was Morris Breen and his dray. He hauled for almost all the businessmen of the city, told his funny stories to the boys when he loafed, and like a true philosopher, extracted all the brightness that was possible out of life and kept the clouds away as long as possible.
>
> Then there came a day when he felt old age creeping on him and his health gave way. He gave up his dray line and

retired from active business. Did he repine and lose any of the jovial characteristics that had so long made him an unique character in the city? Not he. He kept up his spirits to the end, and when he finally left his old friends with whom he had associated so many years he lifted his hat to them and said good-by with a smile and a nod for old memories.

Mr. Breen was about 70 years of age. He had been in failing health for several years and death was probably due to old age. In the passing of Morris Breen another well-known character, whose like we shall not soon look upon again, is gone.

Xenia newspaper, May 1, 1906.

Maurice's son, John (my grandfather), didn't last long in school. After having his ears soundly boxed by his second grade teacher for teasing one of his classmates, an incident that left him with permanent hearing loss in his left ear, he never returned.

One of my grandfather's earliest memories was when he was about five years old and traveled to Columbus, Ohio with his father. The date was April 29, 1865, and they had heard that the funeral train of the late President Abraham Lincoln was passing through on its way to Springfield, Illinois. John remembered waiting in a long line at the State House, slowly walking past the casket, and then the long, tiresome wagon ride home to Xenia.

John worked for the gas company when he was older, lighting the gas street lights of Xenia in the early evening and extinguishing them early each morning. In December 1872, his mother, Mary, died of typhoid fever and his father, Maurice, was left to raise the young family; Maurice never remarried.

THE BECKMANS

Henry Beckman emigrated from Wallenhorst, Germany at the age of 17 in 1849 with only the clothes on his back. His first job was working in a tailor shop. After marrying, he worked hard, saved his money and finally bought out the owner of the shop. During the Civil War, Henry Beckman invented a process to mass-produce clothing and won a contract with the Union Army. His process revolutionized the industry, making him one of the wealthiest men in Cleveland almost overnight.

Henry Beckman, circa 1880.

Army uniforms up to this point were highly variable with local regiments often designing their own. For example, a fad that raged at the time were the Zoauve units, whose leader modeled his troops and their uniforms after the French Foreign Legion. It was no wonder that the Union Army sought a consistent look for its soldiers in order to improve battlefield performance. A key development was Henry Beckman's ability to guarantee that all uniforms would be a consistent shade of blue, something the army had never had when uniforms were manufactured in a variety of locations.

In time, his factory took up an entire city block, becoming known in Cleveland as the "Beckman block." In fact, Henry became so wealthy that an upstart oilman came to him requesting that he partner with

Louisa Erhard Beckman, circa 1880.

him and help finance a new enterprise. Henry turned John D. Rockefeller down flat, saying he didn't invest in things he couldn't "see, feel, or smell." Ironically, many years later and a few states away (Maine), several of the two men's grandchildren became good friends.

Henry Beckman died in 1887 leaving the family a bequest of over $900,000, a fortune at the time and equal to over $18,000,000 today. It not only financed his immediate family's lifestyle, but also made possible education, travel, and numerous adventures for his future grandchildren, among them my father and his siblings.

Henry's wife, Louisa Erhard, was born in Bethlehem, Pennsylvania, the child of immigrant German parents, Sebastian and Teresa, who moved to a farm near Cleveland when Louisa was in her teens. She

Herman Beckman, 1884.

became active in charity work during the Civil War using scrap material from her husband's company to sew bandages. Henry gave Louisa and her friends a room at the factory for their work, and this project began a lifetime of charitable service for her. In 1898, she and two of her daughters, Hattie (now married and living in Toledo) and Katherine (also married and living in Dayton), started the Leonarda Society, the first Catholic hospital auxiliary in Cleveland and the second oldest Catholic social service organization there, to make sponges and bandages for hospital use.

Always a very social individual, Louisa encouraged her daughters to attend finishing schools, took them to Europe, and helped them

*The Beckman children circa 1887. Front row: Teresa, Louise, Henry, Jr.,
and Henrietta (Hattie). Standing: Katherine, Anna, and Josephine (Jo).*

develop native fluency in both German and French. Their German fluency was helped by Henry's father, Herman, who lived with them in his later years and who never spoke English; and Louisa's father, Sebastian, who also lived with them for a time in his later years and who mostly spoke his native German.

In 1895, Louisa and Henry's daughter, Anna, married John Ohmer (who went on to invent the taxi meter) and moved to Dayton, where her new husband resided. Her younger sister Katherine came to visit and met my grandfather, John Breen, who was by then one of Ohmer's business partners. As a young man, John Breen knew all the train engineers passing through Xenia and listened to their stories of faraway places. It was there that John Breen met John Ohmer and Tom Taggart (who later moved to Indiana and founded the famous resort, French Lick Springs, before becoming the political boss of Indiana). In the mid-1890s, John Breen left Xenia and moved thirty miles west to Dayton, Ohio, to work in the hotel and restaurant business with John Ohmer and his brothers. They and John Breen, owned restaurants at train depots from Chattanooga to Chicago. Train engineer friends of theirs would tell them where new track was to be laid and where the refueling stops would be,

The Beckman family home at 44 Ontario Avenue in Cleveland. The two portions of the home were connected by a breezeway in the rear, and the back portion of the house was considerably larger. Various members of the Beckman family lived here from about 1864 through the 1920s. The house was torn down in the late 1930s. Daughter Josephine lived in the corner home portion, photo left.

allowing these farsighted entrepreneurs an early opportunity to open their restaurants and hotels.

John and Katherine got along well. She told him that if he was ever in the Cleveland area, he should stop by for a visit and she would make him an old-fashioned sauerkraut dinner. The very next weekend, Katherine was surprised and flattered to find this same charming and hard working young man standing nervously at the front door of her family's home on Ontario Avenue—one of America's most prestigious addresses at that time. It was a stark contrast to John's modest, wooden home next to the railroad tracks back in Xenia, Ohio. Katherine hurriedly prepared a meal and afterward John took her out for a ride in a horse and buggy. During the ride he impulsively asked her to marry him, and to his surprise and delight, she agreed. When they returned to Katherine's home and he was putting away the horse and buggy, the horse fell over dead.

Katherine Beckman at age 20 (left) with her 16-year-old sister Hattie on vacation in Hot Springs, Arkansas in 1891. The family vacationed there annually, traveling from Cleveland in style on a private railway car.

For the rest of his life, John would joke, "The horse heard my marriage proposal and died of shock!"

On January 18, 1896, John Breen and Katherine Beckman were married at Saint Peter's Church in Cleveland. The Cleveland *Evening Herald* dutifully reported on the morning ceremony, taking care to note that, "The bride is the daughter of the late Henry Beckman, one of Cleveland's well-known and wealthiest citizens. She is a lovable young woman, and a great favorite with a large circle of friends in this city and in Dayton . . ." The article also noted that, "The groom is one of Dayton's popular and prosperous young businessmen."

Aunt Jo

Anna and Katherine Beckman had an older sister, Josephine, always known as Aunt Jo, who became a widow at age 43. My father often related Aunt Jo's story, but his sister MaryLouise's version was definitely more colorful:

She had a Victorian refusal to pull herself out of the slough of her mourning for her still young husband, and much later, I used to hear weird tales of her activities to keep her grief alive. The room he had used was untouched, the chair where he sat was never sat upon. Indeed, according to her sworn reports, it used to rock gently to assure her that John [Callaghan] was present but unseen. Her grief ran an erratic and volcanic course for years wherein she made rather a nuisance of herself to a good many people, and then, all of a sudden, she had a slight stroke which paralyzed her body for a short time but seemed to activate her mind.

When she recovered, she went to Hawaii for a trip, a little plump widow, not young by then, in widow's weeds of the rankest variety.

When the telegram announcing her return arrived, her daughter went to California to meet her and sat in the appointed hotel lobby watching guests come and go. She was accosted finally by a familiar voice. It was the only familiar thing. Gone was the flowing black, replaced by a garish flowered and figure-clinging print. There was, shockingly, a shingled head, and to add to the chamber of horrors, a long, flashy cigarette holder with a steaming cigarette.

Aunt Jo took up residence in an apartment hotel in our city. She had come to the conclusion that life was fleeting and life should be enjoyed. And enjoy it she did, sometimes to the consternation of her more conservative sisters.

She besieged her brothers-in-law for introduction to "rich old men" and was avidly interested in the marital state of almost any male name mentioned in any connection.

Once, while staying at a luxury hotel, an old man slipped a note under the door of her room. It read, "For me to sin is indeed a rarity. For you to sin with me would be a charity!" Aunt Jo replied with a note of her own, "For me to sin is indeed no rarity, but I sin for cash and not for charity!"

Aunt Jo usually wintered in Florida or southern California. She adored silent screen star Rudolf Valentino and happened to be in California when he died in 1926. (He died in New York City but was transported back to Los Angeles for burial.) She bought a very large funeral wreath, rented a limo, and had the driver pull in behind the other cars. Aunt Jo was escorted into the funeral with the family by an oblivious guard, sat in the front row, and even stood in the reception line. According to the stories, she was as upset about Rudolf Valentino's death as she had been about her own husband's.

Left to right: *Josephine (Jo), Anna, and Katherine Beckman around 1886 John H. Ryder, photographer.*

Family lore has it that a famous photo taken at the funeral and appearing in newspapers around the world identified most of the mourners, save a lone "mystery woman". We like to think she was our Aunt Jo.

The Phillips House Hotel was the most elegant hostelry in Dayton, Ohio at the turn of the 20th century. Photo circa 1920, courtesy Marvin Christian Collection.

Before John married Katherine, the second grade drop-out admitted to her that he could not read or write and didn't know proper social etiquette. Always willing and eager to learn, and aware that he needed such skills to succeed in the world, he asked her to be his tutor. Throughout his life, John always told his children and friends that a man should never be too proud to admit not knowing something, nor unwilling to learn a new skill, a moral lesson he imparted by example over the years. While his offspring would have been comfortable in any event thanks to his entrepreneurship and hard work, there is no question that Henry Beckman's contribution provided them (and by extension, John) with polish and social position to a degree they might not have achieved otherwise.

One year after their marriage, John was appointed receiver of the Phillips House Hotel at the corner of Third and Main streets in Dayton,

Ohio. Hotels at this time were significant institutions in their cities. As A. K. Sandoval-Strausz has noted in his 2007 book, *Hotel/An American History*, hotels are an American invention that were seen as serving the cause of democracy and an expanding, mobile, mercantile and increasingly industrial nation. Sandoval-Strausz states:

> *Accommodating so many guests made hotelkeeping an exceptionally difficult business; it was no accident that in nineteenth-century parlance, the expression "he can keep a hotel" meant that the person was extremely capable.*

Competition was fierce among hotels, and successful management demanded a balance between the economics of the hotel itself (staffing, purchasing, accounting, etc.) and attracting the public. It wasn't enough to put "heads in beds;" an upscale hotel such as The Phillips House had to be perceived as an essential part of the community, a place where businessmen and government leaders congregated, women could eat out publicly and in safety, and where a family might choose to celebrate important moments. In addition, overnight guests needed to be repeat guests as much as possible; word of mouth was critical for success. The hotel manager was running a miniature ship of state, occupying a place in community life beyond the mere "managing" of an inn.

The Phillips House, almost a block long and four stories high, first opened on October 14, 1852. It was built by J. D. Phillips and named in honor of his father, H. G. Phillips, a well-known local businessman. It was the most elegant hotel ever built in Dayton and would remain so for seventy-four years, until it was torn down in 1926.

The Phillips House hosted many famous figures during its years of operation. Six years before young John Breen viewed Lincoln's casket, Abraham Lincoln visited the Phillips House. In September 1859 Illinois Senator Stephen A. Douglas, whose campaign debates with Lincoln garnered widespread public attention, stopped at the Phillips House. Less than a month later, Lincoln, accompanied by his wife, Mary, and their young son, Tad, also visited. Mr. Lincoln gave an impromptu speech from the front of the hotel before going in to register.

According to Lloyd Ostendorf's book, *Mr. Lincoln Came to Dayton*, Dan Medler, a young man having lunch in the dining room at the same time, wrote in his diary,

This bed was in the Phillips House Hotel guest room where Abraham Lincoln stayed; Edward G. Breen and his siblings were born in the same bed and it remains in the Breen family today.

Sat., Sept. 17, 1859. The Hon. Abraham Lincoln of Illinois, who was defeated for the United States Senate last fall by S. A. Douglas, arrived at the Phillips House today at noon and in the company with Hon. R. C. Schenck of this place, Hon. Mr. Gurley of Cincinnati, and our would-be Senator Cuppy occupied a table, all by themselves, enjoying their wine and their jokes very extensively.

Others in the hotel that afternoon said that Mr. Lincoln appeared to be in an upbeat state of mind. Annie Harries, the young daughter of state senator John Harries, asked Mr. Lincoln to sign the inside cover of her small pocket Bible. Mr. Lincoln wrote, "Dayton, Ohio Sept. 17, 1859 Miss Annie Harries—Live by the words within these covers and you will [be] forever happy. Yours truly, A. Lincoln." It was one of the few Bibles that Lincoln signed in his lifetime.

Many famous actors and actresses stayed at the Phillips House, including Edwin Forrest, John McCullough, and Edwin Booth, the

John and Katherine Breen in the front seat of the Beckman family carriage. It was this carriage that was involved in the accidental death of Henry Morse Breen; the photo was taken shortly before the accident on April 30, 1899.

brother of actor and Lincoln assassin John Wilkes Booth. Charles Stratton, commonly known as General Tom Thumb (the midget made famous by P. T. Barnum), was reported to have stayed there. Additionally, many Union generals, both during and after the Civil War, stayed at the Phillips House, notably General James Garfield, who would go on to become the twentieth president of the United States.

The Phillips House had many managers over the years, but John Breen was the last, and perhaps the one who was employed the longest, serving for thirty years. Under his careful management, the Phillips House flourished. As new technologies were introduced, the hotel boasted a telephone in every room and a large neon light in front advertising its name. Farmers from outlying areas making day trips to Dayton to sell their produce would stay in town for dinner and wait for nightfall to see this novel attraction blink on and off.

In 1898, John and Katherine had their first child, Henry Morse Breen, born in the same bed at the Phillips House that the Lincolns had once occupied. Many guests at the hotel remembered with delight John bringing his young son into the lobby.

Katherine Breen with her first son, Henry Morse in 1898.

But the happy times were not to last. On sudden notice, John and Katherine were summoned to Cleveland with the news that Katherine's mother, Louisa, was very ill and might die; it wasn't Katherine's mother who perished.

The front page story in the *Dayton Daily News* told it all [note: "Breen" was misspelled as "Breene"]:

FELL ON HIS DARLING CHILD AND CRUSHED HIS LIFE OUT LIKE A FLASH. APPALLING ACCIDENT BEFALLS JOHN BREENE'S BOY. The Dayton friends and acquaintances of Mr. and Mrs. John P. Breene of this city were shocked beyond measure today by the announcement that their 15-month old son had been killed in an accident at Cleveland last evening at 5 o'clock. The intelligence was confirmed by telephone in every particular today. Mr. and Mrs. Breene and Mr. and Mrs. J.H. Edwards of Cleveland and Mr. J.F. Ohmer of this city were out driving in Gordon park in a double seated carriage. Mrs. Edwards was accompanied by her two months old baby while Mr. Breene was in charge of his young son. While driving on the road near the shore of the lake the horses became frightened and almost turned the party into the water. Messrs. Edwards and Breene managed to guide the horses away from the edge of the drive, but in so doing the carriage ran into a sprinkling cart standing in the road. After much excitement and considerable difficulty the animals were stopped and Mr. Breene who held the baby in his arms, started to alight from the carriage when he slipped and fell. He fell upon the baby who was injured seriously. The child was hurriedly conveyed to Leonard's pharmacy at Lewiston Ave. and Saint Clair Street and all efforts were made to revive the boy, but despite medical aid, death ensued. The body was brought back to Dayton and buried at Calvary Cemetery.

Katherine never told her ailing mother what had happened, and Louisa continued to ask to see her grandson until her own death from breast cancer on June 11 of the same year. Katherine never forgot her mother's agony; the "treatment" was the application of a red hot poker on the cancerous spot.

As tragic as Henry's death was, the death of children at a young age was common at the time. Katherine and John were brokenhearted, but

Christmas, 1908 in the manager's apartment at the Phillip's House Hotel. Eddie Breen, seated on his nanny's lap, was born on June 10 of that year.

soon had another son, John, Jr., born in 1900; a daughter, MaryLouise, born in 1904; and finally, my father, Edward (Eddie), born in 1908.

§

My father spoke his first sentence around the age of two and a half. He was looking out the window of their apartment in the Phillips House when he said, "Ain't many much mans out on the street today, Mama." The sentence was humorous because the word "ain't" was forbidden in their family, thanks to Katherine's training.

A favorite game of John's children was to catch their father saying "ain't." If they did, he had to put a quarter in a jar. After enough quarters were collected, the family spent the money on something fun. Katherine also put quarters in the jar every time her husband shaved at home rather than going to the barber shop, as was the custom at the time. Finally, after fifteen or sixteen years of saving quarters, Katherine told

John that they had saved enough to buy a car. Delighted, John arranged to have one delivered from the factory in Detroit.

There were not many cars on the road in 1914. So three weeks later when it was delivered and the salesman parked it by the curb in front of the Phillips House, a large crowd soon gathered. John and Katherine sat in the front seat and John Jr., MaryLouise, and Eddie, as he was always known, climbed into the back. The salesman stood on the running board and gave instructions to John. When it was finally time to give the car a test ride, the crowd stood back. John put the car into gear and it immediately jumped the curb, shot across the sidewalk, crashed through the glass window of a flower shop and slammed into the back wall. The entire time, John was pulling back on the steering wheel and yelling "whoa, whoa, whoa!" as if it were a team of horses. Unfortunately, he never did become entirely comfortable with driving.

John's friend, James Cox, was in his first year as Ohio governor in 1913, also the first year that cars were issued license plates in the state. The governor gave the first 1,000 to his friends and associates, issuing John number 783. Upon John's death, the number passed on to Eddie, and upon his death, to his widow, my mother, who still has license number 783 on her car—just as John had almost a century ago.

There were very few places for fine dining in Dayton, but the Phillips House restaurant was considered one of the best, mostly due to John Breen's skills as a manager. The wait staff was properly trained and the food was prepared to the highest standards. Furthermore, everyone with whom he came into contact understood that John Breen had little room in his life for the racial prejudice that was typical in the early 1900s. It was not uncommon in this era to draw the attention of a waiter by any means, even with words now considered racist. This was not permitted at the Phillips House. Customers were required to summon their waiters, black or white, by first or last name, beginning each with "Mister." A customer could say, "Waiter," but anything less was simply not acceptable. John instructed all his waiters that if a customer did not refer to them in this manner, they were not to respond, and if the customer protested, John would ask them to leave. In a city the size of Dayton, hotelmen talked amongst themselves and if a person was thrown out of one establishment, it was likely that he or she would not be accepted elsewhere in town. Customers quickly learned to respect the Phillips House rules to prevent such embarrassment.

My father remembered an incident that happened when he was eight years old. He, my grandfather, and a friend were sitting in the family car waiting for Tom, the hotel handyman, to drive them to the circus. After a while, my father's friend turned to him and said, "I wish that stupid n---- would get out here." John turned to my father and said, "Eddie, go inside and tell Tom that we don't need him. We'll walk to the circus today." When my father began to protest, saying they would be late if they walked, John replied, "I don't care if we're late or not, I will not have Tom drive someone to the circus who feels that way about him." John knew all too well the discrimination that surrounded the Irish, and he had no desire to visit it upon anyone else.

§

In the early 1900s, Dayton had a population of 85,000. It was Ohio's fifth largest city and it ranked first nationally in the number of patents issued. As the Wright brothers were preparing for their first aeroplane flight, the residents of Dayton, perhaps not grasping its importance, complained of having to wait longer to have the brothers repair their bicycles.

Because all the citizens of Dayton knew each other and there was very little crime, my father's parents never really feared for the safety of their children. When my father was a toddler, John and Katherine would take him across the street to the courthouse lawn, tie a long rope to the cannon, and attach the other end to his waist. This allowed him to play while they worked in the hotel. It was a perfectly safe thing to do and everyone in town would come by and talk to him. One park regular, a man named Sam who sold peanuts from a cart, would give my father free peanuts to throw at the birds, hoping to entice people to buy his product.

§

Back in 1898, John Ohmer had turned to his brother-in-law, my grandfather, whose depot restaurants had become very profitable over the years, for financial backing in order to form a company for his fare meter invention. John agreed to provide the financial backing and join the company as a silent partner. The Ohmer Fare Register Company became very successful, and taxi meters were soon sold across the United States and throughout the world.

In 1911, John Breen took time off from managing the Phillips House to accompany John Ohmer to Europe. While in London selling their

*Cover of Phillips House Thanksgiving menu from 1907 with drawing
and hotel insignia (including John Breen's name as manager).*

taxi meters, they heard about a new ship named the *Titanic* under construction at the Harland and Wolff shipyard in Belfast, Ireland. Supposedly, she was to be the grandest ship ever built. To celebrate their
business success, they decided to come home in style and booked passage months before her departure. In a lucky twist of fate, high sales
for their meters forced them to extend their stay abroad. They canceled
their tickets for *Titanic's* maiden voyage and instead purchased tickets
for her second. After the *Titanic* sank on April 10, 1912, the two men
came home on another ship—not unhappily, under the circumstances.

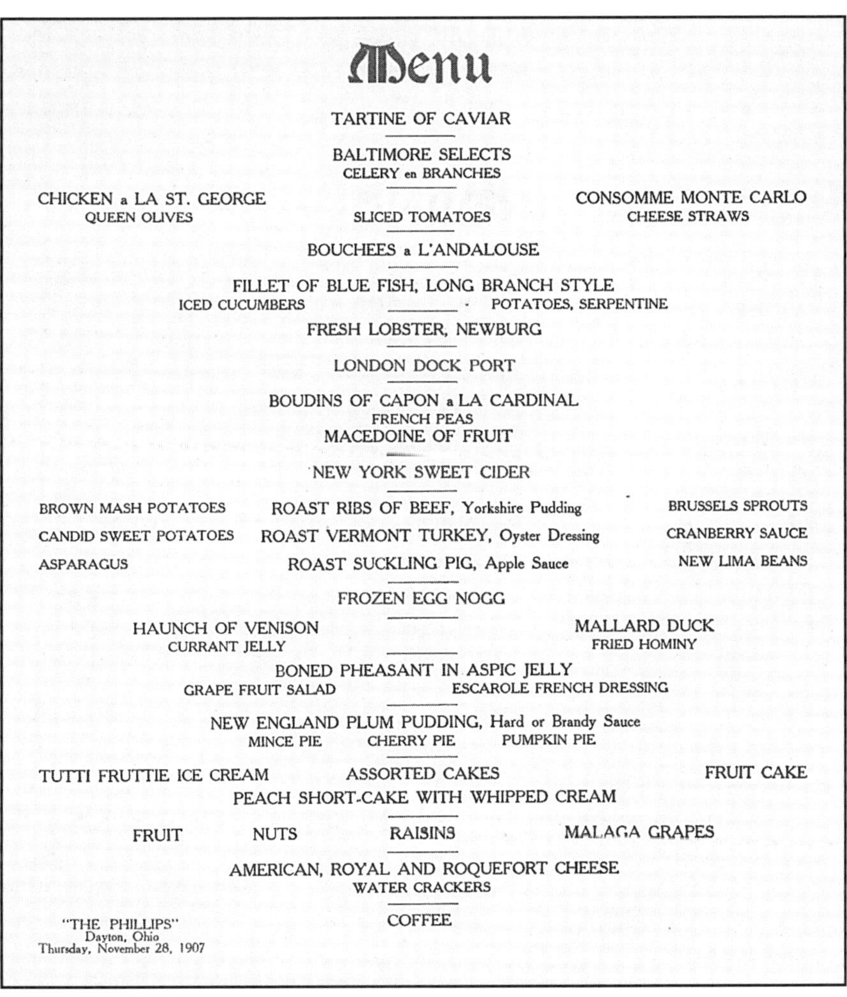

Phillips House Thanksgiving menu from 1907.

The Ohmer Fare Register Company did well for many years, and eventually branched off into making cash registers. However, John Patterson, the known-to-be-ruthless head of the National Cash Register Company (NCR—also based in Dayton), warned them not to compete against him. There were even rumors suggesting that he would ruin them financially if they continued. In time, John Breen realized it would be very difficult to have a successful future with the Ohmer Fare Company, so despite the awkwardness of leaving his brother-in-law's business, he sold his interest to a third party. Ohmer was furious. Within a year, the Ohmer Fare Register Company collapsed, and the Ohmer family lost a tremendous amount of money. As the years passed, feelings healed and the men renewed their friendship; through profits from his other inventions, the Ohmer family eventually recovered from their financial losses.

Independence Day

In the early twentieth century, the Fourth of July holiday was usually spent on the grounds of the Dayton Veterans Hospital. The large grounds included several lakes and many gardens. Families would arrive early in the morning and remain until nightfall. Local veterans from the Civil War and the Spanish-American War held an annual parade, and bands played throughout the day. At noon, there was an annual pie-eating contest, and women entered their picnic baskets to see who had brought the best dinner. A fishing contest and other games were held in the afternoon, followed by a dance in the evening. The day would end with a large fireworks display. Mainly, though, it was a time to visit with veterans and thank them for defending their country. According to an article from the *Lincoln Herald, Commemorative Issue 1897-1997*, Ohio sent more men to fight in the Civil War than any other state, and Montgomery County alone sent 5,896 young men. Many of the veterans would tell their families and friends stories of the battles in which they had fought, among them Stone Mountain, Cold Harbor, Shiloh, Gettysburg, and Vicksburg. Spanish-American War veterans told of their experiences in Cuba. My father first gained his knowledge and love for history as a child on the grounds of the Veterans Hospital, delighting especially in tales told by an old Zoauve soldier who had fought in the Civil War.

Flood of 1913

One evening in late March 1913, John and Katherine left the hotel to go for a walk along the banks of the Miami River, which runs through Dayton. The snow had melted rapidly that spring and combined with continuous rain, the river was dangerously swollen. John noticed that the water level was much higher than normal, and that the ground felt "very squishy," as he recalled years later. The river began to overflow that same night, and when my father looked out of his second story bedroom window the next morning, he saw rising water everywhere. The rooms at the Phillips House began to fill up as people were evacuated from other locations. Fortunately, salesmen and other business

Illustration of the Dayton flood at its height. The Phillips House Hotel can be seen in the distance on the right with (barely visible) people standing on the roof. Illustration by Henry Ellsworth from the Dayton Flood Book Co. Commemorative Booklet, *Dayton, Ohio. This image came from artist renderings of the flood displayed in San Francisco in 1915.*

people who would normally have kept it full had headed home for the Easter holiday. However, as the river kept rising and overflowing, the stream of the displaced became more than a trickle, especially after the earthen dam broke. Dormitories lined with cots were set up in the sample rooms where the salesmen normally showed their wares. As the refugees continued to arrive, cots spilled into the broad hallways.

There was no shortage of personal drama, either. A woman nearing the end of her pregnancy gave birth at the hotel, and a young man suffering from spinal meningitis was brought in on a litter.

Katherine and the family nursemaid escorted John Jr., MaryLouise, my father, and several female guests to the roof of the hotel where they remained for several days.

My father and his siblings never forgot peering over the edge of the hotel roof and seeing frightened horses swimming alongside floating debris. They watched a dining room table float by, complete with tablecloth, cups and plates. A streetcar stopped in front of the hotel slowly

This often-reproduced photo of the 1913 flood shows a sight that the Breen and other children never forgot—desperate horses trying to swim for safety. Unfortunately, many of them didn't make it. Courtesy Dayton Public Library.

filled with water and disappeared. One night, just before sunset, the children heard an elderly black man on a nearby rooftop playing the hymn *Nearer My God to Thee* on a trumpet.

The rising waters weakened buildings and sparked fires from downed and snapped utility lines. As the floodwaters hit the corner of the hotel with full force, John stationed bell boys armed with poles at the long windows to try and direct the full impact of the debris away from the building.

The nearby Beckel House caught fire and John organized his hotel workers and guests to protect the wooden Phillips House from the Beckel's smoldering debris. MaryLouise recalled that the angriest she had ever seen her father was when she walked down a hallway with him about two days into the flood and they discovered three guests at the end of the corridor trying to cook an egg over two candles. John was furious and made them immediately extinguish the flame.

The family later learned that the water had crested at seventeen feet and the hotel had been surrounded by eight major fires. At the time,

The Breen family circa 1913. Front: left to right: Eddie, Katherine, and MaryLouise. Back: John P. and John B.

John and Katherine gathered and knotted sheets into a rope so they could tie the family together. If the hotel gave way and they drowned, they wanted the bodies to be recovered as a group. Fortunately, the Phillips Hotel held. Still, John explored other nearby buildings by traveling over rooftops and when he deemed one a surer shelter, the family fled there. MaryLouise, nine at the time, wrote later that she thought it "great fun to cross the roofs on a narrow plank," a statement that more or less summed up her try anything approach to life.

For security, John, many of the hotel workers, and some of the male guests measured the depth of the water inside the hotel every few hours and looked for cracks in the foundation. At one point during the flood, my grandfather went to his office to store papers in his safe. When he opened the office door, he saw that the safe had fallen through the water-soaked wooden floor. [Author's note: The missing guest book that Abraham Lincoln would have signed when he was a guest at the Phillips House in 1859 was most probably stored in this safe and destroyed in the flood.]

To fight their boredom, John, Jr. devised a way to entertain his frightened younger brother. He turned a large wooden bowl from the hotel kitchen into a sailboat, and using a mouse from his menagerie of pet mice as the sailor, dropped it from a second story window. The swift current carried the boat quickly away. Their father was not pleased to hear of his children's antics, and sent them back to the rooftop with instructions to stay out of trouble.

Over the next few days, John Patterson's National Cash Register Company hastily assembled boats to rescue stranded residents. But the Breen family never asked to be rescued, and waited out the entire flood. Five days later, after the waters finally receded, the city was covered in mud and a strong rancid smell permeated the air. Fearing disease, John Breen sent his wife and children outside the city until the town was safe again. Governor James M. Cox placed Dayton under martial law and sent armed guards to patrol the streets to protect against looting. All told, over 300 people died and more than 1,000 homes were destroyed.

MaryLouise recalled that the experience gave rise to the slogan that was used for many years by the Community Chest in its annual fund drive: "Remember the prayers you said in your attic."

> ### *Katherine Beckman's*
> ### *Dandelion Wine*
>
> *3 quarts perfectly fresh dandelion heads*
> *1 gallon pure spring water*
>
> *Set aside for three days and three nights; then strain through a cloth. Add 3 lbs. of granulated sugar. Then add in the juice from two lemons and two oranges and 1/2 cake of yeast. Put the mixture in a stone jar and let it remain four or five days and nights, or longer if it's still working. Skim off and strain through a cloth. Bottle and label it.*

PROHIBITION

Katherine learned to make peach brandy, dandelion wine, and other alcoholic drinks in order to keep certain customers at the hotel happy after Prohibition began in 1920. Because it was time consuming, she didn't make much, but what little she did helped to keep the hotel in business. Even in the years after Prohibition, she occasionally made her favorite recipes to keep on hand for small dinner parties. Her dandelion wine recipe is still shared among the family.

During this era, the family began vacationing in Canada for a few weeks every summer. Before returning home, they would stock up on liquor to augment what little Katherine produced in her basement. On one such trip, they were stopped at the border and asked by a customs agent to open their suitcases. John stayed in the car while Katherine stepped out and went to the trunk. As she pretended to have a difficult time opening her suitcase, the customs agent finally said, "It's okay, Ma'am, I know a nice lady like you wouldn't be doing anything that was against the law. You remind me a lot of my own dear mother." Katherine thanked him very much for the compliment, got back into the car with her husband and daughter, and they drove off smiling, liquor intact. John observed that in spite of his wife's professed conservatism, she waited until she had a cocktail before she preached prohibition.

Postcard from about 1910 of the Union Depot in Marion, Ohio
where John Breen owned and operated the hotel and restaurant.

Boy Scouts, Part I

Around 1920, my father joined one of the first Boy Scout troops in
Dayton. Scouting started in the United States only in 1910. It was a
very young activity based upon a military model, teaching skills and
attitudes that could later prove useful if and when a young man went
to war. Milton Caniff, who grew up to become a cartoonist well known
for *Steve Canyon* and *Terry and the Pirates*, was a fellow scout and good
friend who used many local people, including my father, as inspiration
for his cartoon characters.

The Front Porch

In 1920, John Breen took his son to Marion, Ohio to check on
another hotel and restaurant that John owned. (While John managed
the Phillips House, the many establishments that he owned along the
train lines in Tennessee, Kentucky, Buffalo, Chicago and other locations
were managed by relatives.) As they were walking down the street in
Marion, they met Mrs. Warren G. Harding. Her husband, Senator Harding, was running for president with a "front-porch" campaign, staying
at home in Marion and giving speeches from his own front porch. Mrs.
Harding asked John if his restaurant would cater her dinner parties, and

Boy Scout Eddie Breen in uniform at age 14, 1922, with his dog, Spotty.

The home of Warren G. and Florence Harding in Marion, Ohio. Harding conducted his "front porch" presidential campaign from here in 1920. Courtesy Library of Congress Prints and Photographs Division, LC-DIG-ggbain-08307, from the George Grantham Bain Collection.

he agreed to bring a contract to the house. Upon learning that Eddie was a Boy Scout, she asked him to visit the next evening in uniform and hear her husband give a speech. The next night, Senator Harding was so pleased by Eddie's presence that he asked him to return in a few weeks with more Boy Scouts from his troop and set up a camp site on the back lawn to entertain visitors.

The boys returned to set up their tents, build a rope bridge, demonstrate how to build fires from friction, and cook over an open campfire. It was good publicity for the Boy Scouts and great entertainment for Harding's guests. For several evenings, my father and his fellow scouts served dinner in their best uniforms. When their chores were complete, Mrs. Harding served them the leftovers, and for dessert the boys were given ice cream—a special treat in those days.

One night, the boys were joined by Senator Harding and his vice presidential running mate, Governor Calvin Coolidge of Massachusetts. At one point in the conversation, Eddie asked Governor Coolidge why

Ohio Governor James M. Cox (left) and Franklin Delano Roosevelt (right) announce their candidacy for the United States presidency and vice presidency respectively at the Montgomery County (Dayton, Ohio) Fairgrounds before a crowd estimated at 100,000, August 20, 1920. Courtesy of Special Collections and Archives, Wright State University.

he always had his dog nearby. The governor laughed and said that the dog actually worked for him. When the boys looked surprised, Coolidge said, "If you don't tell anyone, I'll let you in on a secret. Sometimes I get into long-winded conversations with people. When I have trouble getting away from a person, I put my hand behind my back and make a gesture. My dog comes over and jumps on the person. Then I say, 'Oh, I'm sorry about my dog. Let me take him away.' I'm able to leave and go talk to the next person." Governor Coolidge said he and the dog did so well together, no one ever discovered his secret.

Although Governor Coolidge was a quiet man, he enjoyed telling the boys funny stories. After President Harding died in office and Coolidge became president, he was given the nickname "Silent Cal." A famous story that circulated during his presidency was that of a society lady who sat next to the president at a dinner party one night. She reportedly turned to him and said, "I bet my girlfriend that I can get you to say more then three words." He is reported to have replied, "You lose."

In 1920, Harding and Coolidge were competing for the presidency with another Ohioan—Dayton resident James M. Cox, whose running mate was Franklin Delano Roosevelt of New York. Cox was a Dayton native who began in the publishing business with a single paper in Dayton in 1898 at the age of 28. Ten years later, he ran for and served in Congress for two terms, then served as Ohio governor for three two-year terms before his nomination for the presidency by the Democratic party.

John Breen was in a delicate position because Cox was an old friend, and while this remains undocumented, I believe he was the Ohio treasurer of the Cox-Roosevelt campaign (a long-time family story that is highly credible, given John's financial acumen and position on local bank boards). [Author note: Neither Wright State University, holder of the Cox papers, nor the Ohio State Historical Society could locate any information on the matter.] My grandfather told my father not to tell anyone in their hometown of their catering for the Hardings in Marion; the relationship with Harding was nothing more than a business deal. John and Katherine along with their children were often guests at the Cox home, and Cox lunched at the Phillips House almost daily when in town, something he continued to do until the Phillips House closed. At one time, Cox was a long-term resident of the Phillips House. As he ate breakfast, he would call my father over to his table to show him a trick or a game, endearing himself forever to at least one little boy. Roosevelt was frequently in town in 1920 and often joined Cox at the hotel, the informal business and political center of the city. The relationships forged during this era became of lifelong importance, especially to my father and aunt as adults.

When Harding won the presidency, James Cox returned to running his newspaper empire, which is still in existence with a variety of media holdings. Both my father and grandfather had a long association with him, considering him a strong leader with a great sense of humor.

A Religious Divide

In the 1920s, Dayton did not have much serious crime, but one event shocked the town. Walking home from a meeting one night, a Boy

PROTESTANTS
ᴴAVE YOU STOPPED TO CONSIDER?

ᴬcording to Government Records the ROMAN CATHOLICS comprise 16% of the population of the ᴸes. Yet, for many years the Catholics have held from 62% to 80% of **all public offices.** Why? For ᴬs: First, because they are organized and cooperate. Second, because the Protestant public have not given the proper consideration.

In public office--and particularly in judiciary capacities--a man's **religious faith** will **invariably influence** ᴼinions and **decisions.** Is it fair that the views of the 16% should govern the 100%?

WE MAKE NO CHARGE AGAINST THE CATHOLIC CANDIDATES OR OFFICE HOLDERS
They HAVE and WILL further the interests of their contingent.

BUT WE DO CHARGE

16% OF THE PEOPLE SHOULD NOT GOVERN THE OTHER 84%

It is no discredit to the Roman Catholics that they have elected men of their own faith. It is no discredit to the successful candidates that they have served their constituents. But, there are also able men among those of your own faith.

The Protestant Candidates will serve you and the interests of the 100% better and more fairly than will the candidates of the 16%.

POLITICAL AFFILIATIONS mean LITTLE in THIS ELECLION. PARTY LINES are INDISTINCT.
RELIGIOUS AFFILIATIONS MEAN MUCH.

ARE THE 84% TO SUBMIT TO THE JURISDICTION OF THE 16%
ELECT MEN OF YOUR OWN FAITH

JUDGE HENRY L. FERNEDING
is far too active in Catholic Work to be sitting in judgement over Protestants
A Judge must be fair and broadminded

We particularly object to
JUDGE
ROLAND W. BAGGOTT
who altho a Protestant has for years been **sending Protestant girls** to a **Catholic Home for Correction** when a Protestant home was available.

L. F. BUCHER
Candidate for Coroner

is too active a Catholic to hold public office

We particularly object to
JUDGE
ROBERT C. PATTERSON
who has been **advertising** his **Protestant** connections in an effort to gain support, but who fails to mention that his wife is Catholic, that his **children** are being **raised as Catholics** and attend parochial schools.

NON-PARTISAN PROTESTANT LEAGUE

Political handbill circulated in Dayton in the 1920s.

Scout in my father's troop was murdered. The boy's family asked my father if he would be a pallbearer, along with some of the other scouts. The Breens agreed that this would be a fitting gesture, but the next day, two Catholic nuns informed them that it would not be possible. The dead boy was Protestant, and it was forbidden for a Catholic to enter the church of someone from another religion. John replied that the deceased boy had been his son's friend and although he acknowledged the nuns' concern, his son would participate in the funeral. Several hours later, the local parish priest visited with the same message, but in stronger terms. Again, my grandfather repeated what he had said to the nuns. The priest was not pleased, but he thanked the family and left. In such situations, my grandfather used to say that one should follow one's heart and do what is right.

The deep religious divide between Catholics and Protestants in society at that time carried over into politics. A political handbill circulated around town at the time illustrates the tensions. It was an especially hurtful time for the Breens, as the main target (Judge Ferneding) was a cousin (he was married to Aunt Jo's oldest daughter).

O, Canada

My father and his Boy Scout troop went on a trip to Canada in 1920 when he was twelve-years old. The scouts saved their money for almost a year, and when it was finally time to leave, they, the scoutmaster, leaders, parents, and a small band went to the train station. "Canada or bust!" was scrawled in large white letters on one side of the train car and the crowd happily waved the scouts off on their big adventure to the Canadian wilderness. Once in Canada, the scouts met their Native American guides, hiked through the woods, and finally reached a large lake where they pitched their tents. The scouts proceeded to have a wonderful week canoeing, fishing, and hiking.

On their last night, some of the scout leaders started a card game with the guides after the boys had gone to bed. The next morning, the scouts awoke to discover the local guides gone. Their scout leaders didn't play cards very well—they had lost most of the money set aside for traveling home. Always resourceful, the boys struck camp and used their best scouting skills to find their way out of the woods. Upon reaching town, they were supposed to take a boat across Lake Huron. They talked to the captain, who agreed to ferry them at half price. In order to earn even this much money, the scouts entertained the waiting passengers with songs, skits and a scouting demonstration, then passed a hat. Once on board, the boys repeated their program, and one scout, particularly good at starting campfires by friction, actually started a fire on the back deck, causing some of the passengers to panic. The fire was quickly doused.

A circus visit to Dayton circa 1910. The elephant parade along Main Street was popular with children and all Daytonians; it passed directly in front of the Phillips House Hotel. Photos courtesy Larry Sizer.

Eventually, they made it to the Grand Hotel at Mackinac Island, where they had planned to stay. Since they had no money, the manager said they could sleep on the lawn, provided that they set up after dark and left before sunrise. Finally, the troop made it back to Dayton. Arriving early, no one met them at the train station and they were forced to walk home. The parents were furious when they found out what happened to their boys. The incident was a minor scandal in Dayton that summer.

THE CIRCUS . . .

Shortly after the death of their first son in 1899, and in memory of him, John and Katherine began inviting orphans from the local children's home to the Phillips House for lunch and games followed by a trip to the circus. After son John was born in 1900, the tradition continued as part of his birthday celebration, and a local paper described the event one year in this undated and uncited clipping:

Mr. and Mrs. John P. Breen, with their son, John Breen Jr., entertained eighty children from the Saint Joseph's Orphanage Tuesday afternoon. Three large wagons called for the guests at 1:30 and took them to the Gentry dog and pony show at north Main Street and Shaw Avenue, and after partaking of the varied joys offered by the big show there was another ride to the Phillips House, where a party was given. There was a delicious lunch, and each guest received as a favor a toy of some sort. Even the babies were guests at the hotel, although the tiniest folk were not taken to the show. Each year Master John Breen entertains the children from the Orphanage as the celebration of his own birthday anniversary, and today was a most genial young host, and gave his guests one of the pleasures that will never be forgotten by them. Before evening, the long ride home was enjoyed, and, although the little folks were tired, they were all supremely happy.

Another take on the circus

My father's sense of propriety would never have allowed him to relate the following story to his son. However, he did tell my mother, who related it to me as an example of the kind of situation into which only young boys find themselves.

A few months after the Canadian scouting trip, the circus stopped in Dayton en route to its winter quarters in the South. Seeing the advertisements all over town, my father and his friends decided to skip school and attend the opening day. Soon each had saved a dollar and a dime. It cost ten cents to enter the fairgrounds and another fifty cents to see the circus. With the remaining two quarters, the boys planned to see the side shows and buy food. On the appointed day, they went home at lunch time as usual, but instead of returning to school they headed for the circus.

As they waited in line for their tickets, a midget in costume walked over, offering to sell them a picture of the fattest lady in the whole world, completely nude, for only five dollars. That was more than they could afford to spend, but the midget whispered to one of the boys, "If you buy the picture, you can even see her pussy." This was an age of very different sensibilities.

A circus visit to Dayton circa 1910. Photos courtesy Larry Sizer.

The boys were now *very* interested and after the man reassured them that his claims were true, they decided it would be worth their money. The man left and returned a few minutes later with a brown envelope, saying, "I want you boys to swear that you won't tell anyone that I gave you this picture. This is the fattest lady in the world, and she would sit on me and kill me if she ever found out I snuck under the tent and took this. You have to swear that you won't take the picture out of the envelope until you've left the fairgrounds." The boys handed over their hard-earned money.

As they left the fairgrounds, they decided that they would take turns keeping the picture for one week. Excitedly, they tore open the brown envelope. To their disappointment, though, the fat lady, while indeed nude, had her back to the camera and a black cat sitting on her shoulder. To make matters worse, the next day they were each made to stay after school and repeatedly write on the chalkboard, "I will not skip school to see the circus." Luckily, no mention was made of the infamous photo, versions of which are now readily available on the Internet.

Stanley family plot, Woodland Cemetery, Dayton, Ohio.

...And The Gypsies

In addition to the circus, it was common for gypsies to camp near Dayton in the summer months. Gypsies had been coming to the region since 1856 when the king of the gypsies, Owen Stanley, arrived from England and bought farmland in the Dayton area. In addition, Dayton was a major train junction in the late nineteenth and early twentieth centuries, and gypsy troops often followed the circus trains north in the summer and south to Florida for the winter. After Owen and his wife Harriet died, their son and daughter-in-law, Levi and Matilda Stanley, became king and queen, and gypsies from all over the United States made pilgrimages to Dayton. When Matilda died in 1878, an estimated 24,000 mourners from the United States and Canada arrived in their gypsy wagons. Matilda was buried in nearby Woodland Cemetery, along with Owen and Harriet Stanley. Woodland Cemetery is considered the only place in America that is "campo santo," meaning holy grounds, for gypsies.

In the early 1900s, Levi's son, "Sugar" Stanley, became king. Many Dayton families would drive to the gypsy camps to have their fortunes told or their palms read. Whenever police received word that the gypsies had returned, they would admonish the citizens of Dayton to lock their doors and keep a watchful eye. It was said a gypsy woman would often show up at the front door offering to sell the homeowner something or read their fortune while another gypsy would quietly enter the unlocked back door and steal anything of value.

One year, John and Katherine took sixteen year old John, Jr. and a friend to see the gypsy camp and the colorful wagons they had heard so much about. As they drove into the camp a very large gypsy woman, wearing colorful clothing and much gold jewelry, jumped onto the running board of the car. John politely asked if she would step off, as she was frightening his wife. However, the woman insisted on trying to read their palms. After she ignored his second request, which he uttered a little more forcefully, he opened the car door and stepped on the gas. The last they saw, the woman was rolling down a steep hill. John, who was normally very polite and formal to everyone, was said to break out laughing even years later at the memory of this encounter.

The Family "Crest"

My father came home from elementary school one day around 1918 with a simple assignment: he was to report on his family crest in class the following day. Never having heard of such a thing amongst the Breen or Beckman clans, he asked his father about it that night. John P. told his son to "tell that teacher and class that our family crest is a pick and shovel and don't you ever forget it!" My grandfather always remembered that he came from poor Irish and German stock, and felt it was important that his children remember it, too. Around 1950, my uncle, John B. Breen, worked up a mock family crest from John P.'s saying, and we still use it in the family today.

The Breen family crest.

CHARITY TRIPS WEST AND A NEW HOME

Louisa Beckman, my grandmother, Katherine, and the other Beckman children had worked with the Catholic Church since the early 1890s to provide food, clothing, and schoolbooks to Native Americans living in Arizona. Following Louisa's example, Katherine preferred her charity work to have a hands-on approach. It was typical of her to show up in person to make sure that all was going well. Every winter, my grandparents made a trip to the reservations to see that their donations were well-spent. On these trips, they would meet with a group of Catholic nuns and spend a week or more touring.

In 1924, my father, MaryLouise and John Jr., who were tired of living in their small apartment at the Phillips House, decided to buy their parents a house while they were gone. The siblings found a lovely house in Oakwood, a small suburb of Dayton that was a new, growing area at the time, and only one block from the traction (trolley) line that ran from downtown Dayton. After choosing the house, the three arranged to see their family banker, who told them that he had known their father for years and was aware that he said that one day he would like to own a home. The banker agreed to loan them the money, saying he would work something out with their father upon his return. With the help of the Phillips House staff, the children moved all the furniture and personal items from the apartment to their new home before their parents returned home.

*Katherine Breen with some of the people they met on one
of Katherine's annual trips to reservations in Arizona.*

*John, Katherine & MaryLouise Breen with some of the people they met
on one of Katherine's annual trips to Indian reservations in Arizona.*

Several days later, the three went to the train station to meet their
parents, told them they had a surprise, drove them to the new house,
and proudly took them inside. When John saw his furniture, his jaw
"dropped about a mile." Without saying a word, he walked from room
to room, opening doors, turning on sinks, flushing toilets. His children
didn't know if he was happy or not; to them, he seemed a bit angry.
After walking through the entire house, he finally came back downstairs. With a big smile on his face, he said it was the best thing his children had ever done for their parents.

A MEMORABLE MOMENT

When the family moved to Oakwood, they brought a young black
man named Lamoine Polly to work as a handyman and to drive the
family car. Lamoine, who had been with the family at the Phillips House
for several years, was a hard worker with an easygoing personality. He
planned to be a minister one day and spent a great deal of his time in
the evenings reading the Bible. Several months after moving into their
new home, Katherine hired a cook named Clara. She was a short Irish
woman with bright red hair, a thick brogue, and a rather volcanic disposition, as MaryLouise put it, and it didn't take much to upset Clara.

When John and Katherine took their initial trip to Arizona around 1895, they left Dayton by train, but the final leg of the journey to the reservation was still made by stagecoach.

Why Katherine hired her in the first place is anyone's guess. Almost immediately, Clara took a strong dislike to Lamoine, and the feeling was mutual. Clara had been working for about a month when the family was seated at the dinner table one evening. Suddenly, they heard the sound of a pot crashing against the kitchen wall, followed by the shattering of dishes. Lamoine ran into the dining room looking like a scared deer, followed by Clara, who was brandishing a very large kitchen knife. She chased Lamoine around the table several times while the family sat in utter shock and disbelief. Finally, Lamoine ran out the front door and into the yard with Clara close behind. At that point, John followed them outside, where he told Clara to pack her belongings and leave immediately.

Lamoine remained with the family for several more years until he left for school to finish his religious studies. He eventually became the minister that he had always wanted to be, but he never forgot his run-in with the redheaded cook. No one ever knew for sure what caused Clara to react so violently, although years later Lamoine and the family were able to look back at the incident and laugh.

§

John Breen in front of the only house he ever owned, circa 1925.

LOOKING BACK

Years later, my maternal grandfather, Elmer Focke, confirmed for me the stories I had always heard regarding John Breen's toughness. As a young man, Elmer rode the traction (trolley) line past the Phillips House on his way to the University of Dayton (then known as Saint Mary's Institute) and often saw the stern manager looking out the window of the formal dining room. Elmer's two brothers were occasionally hell raisers with biceps as large as professional weight lifters due to their jobs working in the family-owned slaughtering and meat packing plant (they would lift the carcasses of dead hogs onto a conveyer line to be sent on and processed into ham and bacon). Unfortunately, they made the mistake of entering the Phillips House and getting unruly. John single-handedly rousted them, and they weren't welcome in the Phillips House or any of the other better establishments for several years afterward. As Elmer reported, John Breen was not only a smart businessman but "a very tough little Irishman."

SNAPSHOTS OF DAYTON MEN

In the November 7, 1915 the color *Feature Section* of the *Dayton Sunday News*, included a "Snapshots of Dayton Men" feature on John P. Breen, with a caricature of John P. and a descriptive profile:

Caricature of John P. Breen in the Dayton
Sunday News, *November 7, 1915.*

Snapshots of Dayton Men

John P. Breen

John admits he was on the receiving end of a good lickin' for "playing hookey" from school when a boy.

That lickin' must have left a tremendous impression, for careful research has failed to find a single instance of John playing "hookey" from business since those early days.

We have often wondered who started the depot restaurant idea. We haven't found the originator but we have discovered that John has been one of our very best of the improvers on the idea. Not long ago when the conductor yelled "Fifteen Minutes for Lunch" and the travelers "bee lined" it to the station find themselves eating in a place managed by John P. Breen.

John at one time conducted railroad restaurants at Chattanooga, Tenn., Lexington and Somerset, KY, Huntington, Ind., Dayton and Marion, Ohio.

In addition to his work of running the Phillips House he still runs the Dayton and Marion restaurants.

Tom Taggart and John were boy chums in Xenia, Ohio and both got their first real taste of work in the railroad restaurant of that city. It under the management of "Nick" and George Ohmer—John's next job was with the Little Miami Railroad dining room in Cincinnati.

John has reached the golf enthusiasm stage after ten years of coaxing. He used to be too busy to see the golf bug but "like all the rest" once they are bitten—they never get over it.

He is chairman of the committee entrusted with the mission of finding a new home for the G.D.A [Greater Dayton Alliance].

MORE ON THE FOCKES

While my father's and aunt's stories understandably focused primarily on their Breen and Beckman forebears, the Fockes (my mother's family) deserve a note of their own. My grandfather, Elmer (1892-1986), emerged from a rough and tumble clan of meat butchers and packers in Dayton who nonetheless built a successful business that survived for over ninety years. He was the only son to graduate from college, became

Marie Berno as the character Polly in Apple Blossoms
*(above); photo by Harris of Chicago. The musical opened
at the Colonial Theatre in Chicago on August 29, 1920.*

the company's treasurer, spent his career in an office rather than "on the line" hefting hog carcasses, enjoyed the arts, and traveled widely.

During the 1920s, he fell in love with a voice on the radio. Marie Berno (1895-1990) was a successful stage actress who had appeared on Broadway and toured throughout the United States and Europe. She often appeared with Fred and Adele Astaire (where she often danced

---

Colonial Theatre

A. L. ERLANGER and HARRY J. POWERS
MANAGERS
Also Operating Illinois, Blackstone and Powers Theatres

Rollo Timponi, Business Manager
COLONIAL THEATRE

FIRST WEEK

Beginning Sunday Evening, August 2?, 1920

CHARLES DILLINGHAM
Presents

"Apple Blossoms"

An Operetta in a Prologue and Two Acts

Music by FRITZ KREISLER and VICTOR JACOBI
Book and Lyrics by William Le Baron
Staged by Fred G. Latham and Edward Royce

(The book is based on "Un Marriage sous Louis XV.," by Dumas)

CHARACTERS
(In the order of their appearance)

JULIE.....................................MISS RUTH LEE
POLLY...................................MISS MARIE BERNO
MOLLY..................................MISS ADELE ASTAIRE
JOHNNY ....MR. FRED ASTAIRE
NANCY..................................MISS WILDA BENNETT
LUCY FIELDING.................MISS CATHERINE BRENNON
ANABEL MASON ....MISS DOROTHY HAIGHTON
RICHARD (DICKEY) STEWART.........MR. PERCIVAL KNIGHT
CHAUFFEUR...........................MR. HARRY CORNELL
GEORGE WINTHROP GORDON...........MR. MAURICE DARCY
HARVEY.................................MR. EDGAR NORTON
PHILLIP................................MR. JOHN CHARLES THOMAS
MRS. ANNE MERTON...................MISS EDNA TEMPLE

Program Continued on Second Page Following

Colonial Theatre program for Apple Blossoms
with Fred Astaire as the character Johnny *and
Marie Berno as the character* Polly.

with Fred), traveling with them on the cast train car from city to city. Finally, the star-struck Elmer got his wish. He was introduced to Marie in Mansfield, Ohio, her hometown, and they married in Saint Clotilde Church in Paris, France on August 2, 1927.

Marie gave up her career after her marriage, but she always stayed in touch with Fred Astaire, especially treasuring an eightieth birthday card she received in which he wrote, "thanks for the memories."

20TH CENTURY ANTEBELLUM

*Eddie Breen punting on the River Cam while
a student at Cambridge University, 1927.*

In 1927, a year after my father graduated from Saint Mary's Institute (now the University of Dayton), he and his sister, MaryLouise, who had graduated from Saint Mary of the Woods College, left for a one-year stay in England. She was every bit as intelligent, high spirited and adventurous as he, maybe more so, and made for an ideal traveling companion.

They both enrolled at Cambridge University, where he especially liked wearing the Cambridge school uniform and punting on the River Cam. Tourists would ask him to pose for pictures, thinking they were getting a photo of a typical English college boy.

*Eddie and MaryLouise Breen visited these German relatives
from their mother's side of the family (the Beckmanns) during
the 1920s. Johannes is the five-year-old boy in the cart.*

In 1928, after their year in England, the two traveled throughout
Europe, stopping in Germany to visit their mother's relatives. Because
MaryLouise and my father had native fluency in German, they were
able to travel easily. They attended a family wedding and spent several
weeks on the Beckmann family farm in the villages of Wallenhorst and
Osnabrück. [Author's note: The original German spelling of Beckman is
Beckmann.] The American siblings were amused to find that the young
girls and older women still wore traditional wooden shoes. The visitors
brought gifts of beaded belts for their three cousins—Joseph, Johannes,
and Alois—and gave their uncle a silver and turquoise ring. All of these
were handcrafted by the Arizona Native Americans their mother had
visited the prior year. The Beckmann relatives had never seen anything
like these gifts and were amazed that anyone could visit with "wild red
Indians," as they thought of them, whom they believed all lived in tepees
and used bows and arrows. When it was time for MaryLouise and my
father to return to America, the relatives gave them fresh eggs, homemade bread, and sausage to give to their mother, not realizing how long
it would take them to travel.

MaryLouise Breen (in back) was as adventurous as her brother. She made this trip to India circa 1934.

In 1929, no one had any idea that in little more than a decade, America would be at war with Germany once again. Moreover, Captain Eddie Breen and Private Johannes Beckmann, would end up on opposite sides of the lines at the Battle of Anzio where Johannes would be taken prisoner on May 23, 1944.

§

THE BILTMORE

Dad's older brother, John, was formally introduced to the hotel business as a child. At the age of eight, his parents gave him a business suit to wear and small leather brief case to carry while he accompanied my grandfather on his rounds. However, as he grew up, young John realized that he wasn't temperamentally suited for the trade (a short temper and a need to placate guests aren't a good match), so he decided to pursue other avenues, leaving the way open for his younger brother. In the meantime, Eddie remained behind at the Phillips House in the care of his mother and sister where he enjoyed the full benefits of their attention plus constant exposure to the upscale hotel atmosphere.

By his late teens, my father had entered the hotel business like his father before him. In the late 1920s, my grandfather had a disagreement with the owners of the Phillips House and lost his job. John sued the owners and won, which resulted in the owners having to rehire him, as well as my father. The owners, though, found a legal loophole, discovering that they didn't have to place them at the same hotel. For spite, they sent my father to work at the Gibson Hotel in Cincinnati where he worked three stories below ground peeling potatoes and slicing grapefruit every day.

In late 1929, John Breen was offered a job as manager of the Dayton Biltmore, a new hotel in town. Although it had only recently opened, the Biltmore was faring poorly because of the recent stock market crash. John was a natural choice for the job with his proven track record in hotel management, as well as his financial skills.

John would not accept the job unless his son co-managed with him. The Biltmore was one of the fanciest hotels in Dayton at that time, with marble floors, Oriental rugs, crystal chandeliers and dozens of potted palms. As co-managers, the two men always wore tuxedos, the standard of the day.

§

During their first year, at the beginning of the Great Depression, seventeen guests committed suicide. It got to the point that the clerks behind the front desk resorted to black humor, asking one another, "Do you think he wants a room for sleeping or jumping?"

My father was profoundly affected by one such incident. A man came to his office one day asking to talk, but my father, who usually had a sympathetic ear, sent him away, telling him to come back. An hour later, Dad left the hotel; as he stepped outside, the man's body crashed from the sixteenth floor to the sidewalk next to him. As soon as my father realized who the person was, he promised himself that he would never again be so busy that he couldn't take a few minutes to at least make certain that a person wasn't in need of help.

§

The Dayton Biltmore Hotel, circa 1930. Photo by C. M. Bunting.

My grandfather managed the Biltmore with the same fairness and even-handedness with which he had run the Phillips House in years past, and my father learned to do the same. One story they recalled happened about a year into the job after they hired a black bartender. This man was well-known as the best bartender in town; and if my father and grandfather had not hired him, he certainly would have found employment with another establishment.

After this man was on the job for about a month, four of the white waiters in the hotel came into my father's office and demanded that their colleague be fired or else they would quit. When my father asked why, the waiters replied, "Nobody wants to come into the hotel and be served a drink by a black man when there are bank presidents selling apples on the street corner." My father told them that he understood, and asked to have the bartender sent up to his office. When the bartender walked in with downcast eyes, my father asked him, "How many drinks a minute can you make?" The man replied, "As many as you want, Mr. Breen." Then my father asked, "How many different kinds of drinks can you make? The bartender answered, "As many as you want, Mr. Breen." When my father asked how many children he had at home, the man answered, "quite a few." Then my father said, with anger in his voice, "Are you aware that four of the best waiters in this hotel just came to my office and said they can't work with you?" When the bartender replied yes, my father said, "I'd like for you to go back downstairs, find those four men and tell them that you have now been promoted to head of the dining room and that we no longer need them here at the hotel. Then I want you to take the day off, go back to your neighborhood, and find four men that you can work with. Have them back here by 5:00, dressed and ready to serve dinner."

When the owners of the hotel heard, they called my father into a special meeting and insisted he rehire the four white men and fire the black men. My father simply responded, "Gentleman, my father and I took over this hotel last year when it was bankrupt, and in one year's time, we turned it around to earning a profit. Don't come to the Biltmore and tell me how to run the hotel and I won't tell you how to run your bank. If you continue to interfere, I'll quit and you can go back into bankruptcy." The owners backed off and left him alone after that. Many years later, when my father made his first run for public office, this same bartender rallied many of his friends and neighbors, helping ensure my father's victory.

§

The Biltmore was such an important part of Dayton life in the 1930s and 1940s that much of what happened in and around the hotel regularly appeared in the local newspapers, including the story, with the headline: *This Pig Not in Parlor, But Very Much at Home in Hotel*. The story also reveals a bit about attitudes toward Irish-Americans at the time.

Pigs are accustomed to going to market and to staying home, according to the saying, but staying at the hotel while the owner is at market is something new in pig history and in hotel history. Improbably as it sounds, it nevertheless happened at the Biltmore the other day, and this is the tale: Edward Breen, assistant manager of the hotel, was going through the house, as is his duty. He went into one room which he knew for certain was empty. Hardly had he closed the door when he heard a scuffle, a falsetto sigh, followed by one of those to-the-marrow-of-the bone groans. Somewhat unnerved Mr. Breen stood still. Another groan; a series of scuffles. The sound came from the bathroom, and Mr. Breen went thither, opened the door a crack, got his arm in, and flashed on the lights. Looking through the crack he saw the room empty. He threw open the door and leaped aside not knowing what was coming out. Nothing came, except another groan. Finally he entered the room and saw a tiny chilled pig in the bathtub. Its constant shaking made the scuffling sound. The animal was taken downstairs and fed, and to await its owner. Requested to get rid of the pig, the owner shipped it back to Kentucky. He stated that he had taken the pet to Cleveland and New York City hotels, but the management hadn't gotten wise. It had been smuggled upstairs in a suitcase, and how it got there without bell hops hearing it, is still beyond all concerned. The incident was one of those things which happen at hotels, and every hotel, at one time or another has had something equally as queer happen, although every experience didn't cheat the assistant manager out of several years growth. The adage "there was a pig in the parlor and it was Irish too," will now have to be changed to "there was a pig in the bathtub and it was shaking too."

On another occasion, a guest returned to his room after a night of heavy drinking at the hotel bar. As a joke, one of his friends in another room called him on the telephone, pretended to be the manager, and accused him of stealing silverware from the dining room. The angrier the man became, the funnier his friends thought it was. Finally, the man hung up, called the front desk, and demanded to see the manager. My father, unaware of the prank, went to answer the man's complaint. When he walked into the room, the man jumped him from behind the door, stuck a gun to his head and threatened to shoot. Fortunately, two women were also in the room and they begged the inebriated man to put down his gun before anything fatal occurred.

Sometimes, though, fatalities did occur. A gathering of convention-eers was staying on the top floor of the hotel and decided to amuse themselves by filling a large paper bag with water and dropping it from the window onto a crowd of people who were watching a parade on the street below. Instead of soaking the crowd as intended, the bag came down like a ton of bricks, hitting and killing one of the spectators. My father rode to the hospital in the ambulance with the man, and later had the unpleasant task of notifying his wife.

One man who lived at the hotel was an Native American who had retired from riding bucking broncos out West and somehow ended up in Dayton. He would sometimes get very drunk on Saturday nights, and several boys from Steele High School would sneak into the hotel and try to fight him. Hotel security was always called, and the students were always ejected from the hotel. This scenario went on for a very long time. My father said that for some reason, though, he got the impression that the man actually enjoyed the Saturday night fights, though Dad never could be sure. But several years later when the man died, it was revealed that he had made quite a bit of money in his lifetime, and he left it all to one of those boys.

The Kittyhawk Room

The Biltmore added a landmark attraction in 1931 during my grandfather and father's tenure as co-managers. The Kittyhawk room was a beverage and dining room featuring a gigantic mural honoring the Wright Brothers' first controlled manned flight at Kitty Hawk, North Carolina. The room also featured technical advances such as the first use of fluorescent lighting in such a setting, advances that not even the New York and Chicago hotels had adopted yet. It was an instant hit, attracting customers eager to experience the ambiance and to hear first-rate entertainment such as the Jimmy Dorsey Band.

The Kitty Hawk dining room at the Dayton Biltmore Hotel circa 1931.

Hotel World-Review, a trade magazine, described the room:

> ...the most novel feature of the "Kittyhawk" is a ceiling built of 3,700 square feet of plate glass mirror. No other ceiling of its size ever was constructed in this country, according to the glass company which created it. Lighting of the room is another novelty, striking and attractive. It is plain white, in endless tubes around the room, and up and down pillars in the room.
>
> Carpet and furniture upholstering in the room are treated so they will not stain or catch fire from a lighted match or burning ciggie dropped on them. A dance space in the center of the room will accommodate possibly 75 couples at once. The orchestra pit will seat a 16-piece band. Venetian blinds enclose the outer sides of the room and these, too, are in a soft blue that adds more and more richness. Paintings are few, but strikingly unusual in their theme. They breathe the spirit of aviation, for which the world is indebted to Dayton.

Keeping Up Appearances

Hotels of the 1920s and 1930s were very regimented institutions, and employees were expected to work under strict rules. Large hotels were like a city within a city—most had their own security people, doctors were readily available, and many had beauty shops and laundering services. Guests could leave shoes in the hallway at night and an employee would collect them, polish them and return them to the room by the next morning. The Biltmore even offered a service in which the guests could leave coins and dollar bills in a tray, and they would be returned crisp and clean, without a penny missing.

The manager was expected to wear a tuxedo with a fresh flower in the lapel, and to have his nails buffed, hair coiffured, and shoes shined. Since Eddie Breen was unmarried, it was written into his contract that he was not permitted to bring a date to the hotel for dinner or even be seen in the hotel bar with her. When he did have a date (which wasn't very often, as he had very few days off), he had to take her elsewhere in town. It was also his job to recognize the local prostitutes and to keep them out of the hotel. If a hotel got a reputation as one that allowed prostitutes, it would lose its upscale clientele.

Part of the job was to personally greet VIP guests upon their arrival as well as to visit their rooms and personally ensure their stays were satisfactory. Failure to do any of these things could cost him his position. All the while, he had to display impeccable manners, as this was what guests expected from the employees of the finer hotels. The Biltmore consistently demanded all of his attention and energy. But after all, it was the Great Depression, and if a person was unhappy with his or her working conditions, there were many unemployed who would be more than happy to take over.

At one point in the early 1930s, a famous African-American trumpet player came to town to play at the Victory Theater, and requested a room at the hotel. My father had to obtain the owners' consent first. The owners eventually agreed to a compromise, though with many conditions that are abhorrent today. The musician had to arrive after dark and use the freight elevator. He also had to order room service; under no circumstances could he take meals in the dining room. He was told to leave by early morning and all the sheets he slept on were to be thrown out and the carpet replaced. According to my father, the owners even insisted the room number itself be changed. My father did not like any of this, but, as he did not own the hotel, in this instance he agreed to the compromise.

*Eddie Breen circa 1930 at the time he was
co-manager of the Dayton Biltmore Hotel.*

John Dillinger

In September, 1933, my father got a call from a desk clerk saying that a salesman from Indiana wanted to cash a check. My father took a quick glance at the man, and because he looked vaguely familiar, he told the clerk to go ahead and cash it. A Dayton police detective called the next day to tell him that John Dillinger, the infamous bank robber, had been arrested at the boarding house of Lucille Stricker. They asked my father to come down to the police station and identify the man who had written the check at the hotel: his "salesman" was the infamous John Dillinger. Apparently Dillinger had come to Dayton to visit an old girlfriend, Mary Longnaker. My father never forgot his brief encounter with Dillinger and he often recounted the incident when the subject of bank robbers or criminals arose.

Paul Mantz and Amelia Earhart

Dayton was known as an air force town as far back as 1917 with the construction of Wright Field, which became Wright-Patterson Field in 1948. Many test pilots and army officers stayed at the Biltmore in the 1920s and 1930s.

Paul Mantz, a young pilot from California and close friend of Amelia Earhart, tested planes at Wright Field. He also experimented with new instruments designed to aid pilots flying in low visibility conditions such as fog. When visiting Dayton, Mantz stayed at the Biltmore, where he became good friends with my father.

Today, Paul Mantz would be considered an extreme stunt flyer. In his era he was the only pilot in America licensed to fly a plane through a building or under a bridge, something he did in many early movies. He was also a very funny and interesting man to talk to, and my father spent many evenings listening to tales of his daredevil escapades.

Sundays were usually slow in the hotel business, so Dad occasionally had the day off. He and a group of his friends, many of them young pilots staying at the Biltmore, often went to his mother's for dinner where Katherine enjoyed the company of her son and his friends. They all appreciated not only the good food prepared by Bertha, the family's Mennonite cook, but also Kitty's homemade alcoholic beverages, especially her famous dandelion wine. After dinner they would relax and "talk shop." My father and Katherine loved to hear these stories, and Paul enjoyed the dinners because it gave him time to socialize with some of the other pilots outside of work.

1933 Dayton arrest photo of John Dillinger. Photo courtesy of Special Collections and Archives, Wright State University.

In August of 1936, Paul Mantz flew to California to test the Northrop A-17 fighter plane, a two-seater plane used by the army, and to have dinner with Amelia Earhart and her husband, George Putnam. He asked my father to join him on the trip, and Dad eagerly agreed. Katherine and my father's nephew, Johnnie, came to Wright Field to see them off. As they waited for the gas truck to finish pumping, Katherine turned to my father and said, "Since Mr. Mantz is so nice to fly you out to California, you should offer to pay for the gas."

As they flew, Paul radioed my father in the backseat and asked, "Hey Eddie, have you ever seen the Grand Canyon before?" When my father replied no, Paul shot the plane straight down into the canyon and up the other side. My father thought his heart would burst from his chest.

Eddie Breen (in flight suit), two friends, his mother (on his left) and nephew Johnnie, before flying to California to have dinner with Amelia Earhart, August, 1936. The plane is a Northrop A-17. Built originally as an attack bomber for the Army Air Corps, it appears to have been modified for transport, according to the National Museum of the USAF at Wright Patterson Air Force Base in Dayton. The photo was probably taken by Paul Mantz.

Dinner with Amelia Earhart and George Putnam was at the very elegant Renaissance Room in the Biltmore Hotel in Los Angeles. Earhart was leaving shortly for her highly publicized flight around the world and Paul Mantz was acting as her technical advisor. Terri Minor, a woman who was dating Paul at the time and who later became his wife, was also there. Terri's late husband had been a pilot and an acquaintance of my father's; in fact, she and my father had once dated. Terri, who was normally quite talkative, didn't have much to say that night and it appeared as if she and Amelia were not getting along very well. Both women were fond of Paul Mantz, and there was a rift between them as a result.

Amelia, though, was very animated in talking about her upcoming flight. Paul wanted to install a newly developed radio equipment for her plane, but George didn't think it necessary to add the extra weight. Paul Mantz was known for the risks he took and his crazy stunts, but he was also very safety conscious. At one point, my father recalled, the discussion between the two men became rather heated.

Paul Mantz with Amelia Earhart and her Lockheed Vega just prior to the 1934 Bendix Race. Mantz, an accomplished Hollywood stunt pilot, served as her technical advisor from 1934 until she was lost in 1937. The photo is signed by Earhart, Mantz and Mantz's fiancée, Terri Minor, and was given to Ed Breen after their dinner together in 1936. The photo is considered quite rare because Earhart rarely signed them. Courtesy National Air and Space Museum, Smithsonian Institution (SI A-38749).

After Amelia's disappearance, my father often thought of the argument that night between the two men. Paul told him months later that he had never liked her choice of Fred Noonan as her navigator. Paul felt that Noonan's knowledge of the plane's instruments was shaky, and furthermore, Fred was rumored to be battling alcoholism. Others had voiced the same concerns, but Amelia liked Fred and expressed her confidence in his abilities.

For years afterward, some people held Paul Mantz responsible for Amelia Earhart's ill-fated flight, which bothered him deeply. He believed he had done everything possible to see that she was equipped with the latest, most accurate technology, including his urging that Amelia use the newly developed radio equipment (it was not installed because of weight concerns). And, of course, Amelia had been one of his dearest friends.

My father and Paul remained friends for many years. During World War II, they met in Europe and shared a bottle of wine under a sturdy wooden desk during a night of heavy wartime bombing. When the war ended, Paul returned to stunt flying for the movie industry, and eventually started his own company. As always, he took risks that other pilots would not, and became the best in the business. On July 8, 1965, at sixty two years of age, Paul Mantz was killed when his stunt plane broke apart just as he landed in a desert airstrip in Arizona, filming on location for *The Flight of the* .

Hotel Manager

In the early 1930s, the De-Witt chain of hotels acquired the Dayton Biltmore and my grandfather retired. My father was offered a position as assistant manager for the winter months at the Bon Air Hotel in Augusta, Georgia. The Bon Air was one of America's most exclusive winter resorts with golf courses, horseback riding, tennis, polo, and trapshooting. Golf legends such as Bobby Jones and Walter Hagen often played there. In fact, his appointment to the position was so significant that it was written up in the papers and he was described as "a member of an outstanding hotel family."

Dad's first week as assistant manager was nearly perfect. Every night, he was invited to a dinner or social event at one of the lovely antebellum homes in the area and he concluded that life couldn't get much better. After several weeks, though, someone mentioned in passing that he was Catholic. After that, his social life came to a screeching halt. Except in

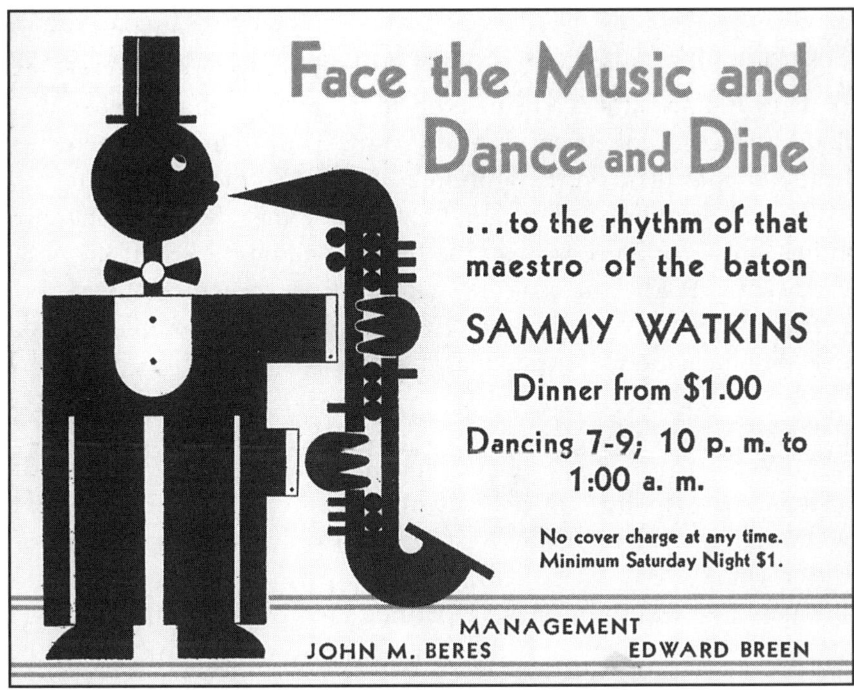

Event announcement listing Biltmore co-managers John Beres and Edward Breen.

the course of business, no one would even converse with him, restaurants would not serve him, and the families that had been so pleasant to him just the week before let it be known that he was no longer welcome in their homes. His only friend during these lonely months was an English housekeeper, and whenever they spent any time together, they had to drive to a different town in order to ensure that his social stigma would not spread to her.

For the first time in his life, my father personally experienced prejudice and he never forgot what it was like. The winter he spent in Augusta turned out to be one of the worst of his life. My father told me that he never understood how such otherwise decent people could feel so much hatred.

Less than a year later, De-Witt went bankrupt and Winter's Bank took possession of the Biltmore. When this happened, my father was recalled from Augusta and hired to co-manage the Biltmore. He worked with a man named John Beres, and the two got along very well. A marketing brochure from that time states, "The Biltmore, with 550 rooms, is excellently managed by John M. Beres and Edward Breen, known throughout the middle west for their hospitality." So they were.

Beres and my father came up with an interesting solution when they had to order place settings and silverware. They didn't know whether to monogram them with "Biltmore", "Dayton Biltmore", "D. B" or just "B". In a sudden burst of insight, they realized that "B" could stand for either Biltmore, Beres or Breen, so they settled on the "B." If the hotel ever went out of business, or they had to update the table settings, both men could use the dishes at home. My mother still gets compliments on her personally monogrammed table settings.

Miss America

Marian Bergeron, the youngest woman to be crowned Miss America, visited Dayton in the mid 1930s after she began touring as a singer. (She was a 15 year-old girl from West Haven, Connecticut when she won the crown in 1933.) My father hired her to perform a cabaret act at the Biltmore and was so impressed that he called Don Ruhlman, a friend staying at the hotel, woke him from a deep sleep, and insisted that he come down and watch. After the show, Marian came to their table and talked to my father and Don. A few days later, when her tour had left Dayton, Don called my father and said, "Remember the show that Miss America put on at the hotel? I followed her home to her parents' house in Connecticut and we're going to get married and move back to Dayton." My shocked father tried to talk him out of it, thinking such a glamorous young woman would never be happy in Dayton. Luckily, he was wrong on this one. They did marry, and lived happily ever after in Dayton. To show their gratitude for bringing them together, Don and Marian frequently introduced my father to her Miss America friends. When the Ruhlmans visited my father years later in Washington, they also included a good friend and fellow congressman on these blind dates—Jack Kennedy.

End of an Era

My grandfather, John, died of cancer at his home in Oakwood in 1936. The following eulogy appeared in a Dayton newspaper:

> John P. Breen has passed on now. His generation of hotel men earned its place in history. They bent the twigs of a fast growing tree in the right direction and that tree was destined to grow to gigantic heights. Then a new day

Marian Bergeron (center), at age 15 the youngest woman ever crowned Miss America. Photo courtesy of the Miss America Organization.

in business dawned. That ruggedness of individualism seemed to pass. What has replaced it may prove some day to be right, too.

But as those venerable old gentlemen of other days put aside the working tools of hotel operation, they leave standing in our midst a creed that yields to no change. In a few words it is: "The Golden Rule."

That's what measured the pace of John Breen's life. It led him to earthly success. It earned him the admiration and respect of his fellow men. It made him a beloved husband and father. It brought him to peaceful sleep in Death.

Several weeks after my grandfather's death, an elderly man knocked on my father's office door, telling him, "I have good news for you. I just heard from your father." Surprised, my father asked what he said. The old man reached into a shoe box, pulled out a crumpled piece of paper and replied, "Your father wants you to know that he is now a dog and living in Cleveland, Ohio. He is very happy and he has a large yard to run around in and he likes his master." Keeping a straight face, my father thanked the man politely and sent him on his way.

THE DAYTON VAN CLEVE

In the late 1930s, my father received an offer from owner Frank Hillsmith to become sole manager of the opulent Dayton Van Cleve Hotel, thus becoming the youngest manager of a large metropolitan city hotel in the United States at that time. Female guests quickly spread word on the hotel grapevine about the handsome eligible bachelor at the helm, adding to the hotel's (and my father's) cachet throughout the Midwest.

In October 1940, an article headlined *The Human Side of It—As Seen by Bert Klopfer* appeared in a Dayton newspaper:

Ed Breen, manager of the Van Cleve hotel is very much in a bad way. That is to say charges have been filed against him by no less an organization then The Barflies. This, let it be said, is any sort of informal organization of business and professional men who meet for lunch, and occasional ice cream, at the Van Cleve daily. The 'charges' are embodied in a 900-word statement filed by " the committee on deficiency, delinquency and inefficiency" and was attested by a 'justice of the peace.' The charges amplified with specifications allege that the debonair Breen doesn't offer the members drinks any more; that he has been seen with feminine companions unknown to the Barfly brotherhood; he has permitted the Van Cleve bowling team to bowl without shirts; has failed to appear with bottle before the austere group and that he has "endeavored to intimidate and humiliate the brothers with his extensive wardrobe and ever-present boutonniere.

The punishment provides that Breen must furnish the members with telephone numbers; put Scotch in Scotch highballs; report at regular intervals his mental, moral, physical and financial condition, and provide lodge rooms of the 'order' with pool tables, cuspidors and shower baths. All of which means there's lots of fun in store for Ed and the other members of the Barfly Club.

Billboard advertising the Dayton Van Cleve in the 1930s. Note the room rate.

The Roosevelt Families

Eleanor Roosevelt, wife of President Franklin Roosevelt, stayed at the Van Cleve during my father's tenure. He remembered visiting the First Lady in her room one afternoon while she was knitting, reading a book, and talking to him simultaneously. She wasn't rude, just an energetic woman who needed to be doing many things at once. Of all the famous guests who stayed at the Van Cleve, my father felt she was one of the most gracious and down-to-earth. For example, when several children arrived and were told they could not ask for her autograph, Mrs. Roosevelt heard of it and immediately came down to the lobby. She signed their autograph books and then treated them each to a bowl of ice cream.

After her stay, my father received a warm thank-you note from the White House, dated July 22, 1940:

My Dear Mr. Breen:

I want to thank you so much for your hospitality and for the lovely flowers which you gave to me. I am deeply grateful for your many kindnesses and my stay at the Van Cleve Hotel was more than pleasant.

Very sincerely yours,
Eleanor Roosevelt.

A dinner dance was held at the Van Cleve on January 30, 1941 in celebration of Franklin Delano Roosevelt's birthday. Captain Elliott Roosevelt was stationed at nearby Wright Field, so the Roosevelts were frequently in town to visit their son and his family, and usually stayed at the Van Cleve. My father was a guest, sitting with the Captain and his wife that special evening.

Alice Roosevelt Longworth was another guest who passed through Dayton from time to time. She was the oldest daughter of President Theodore Roosevelt and the widow of Cincinnati-born former U.S. House Speaker Nicholas Longworth. Prior to his death, whenever she and her husband argued (usually over his drinking), she would leave for Dayton and a stay at the Biltmore. After she was widowed, she continued to visit, this time staying at the Van Cleve, where she always had something amusing to say, re-inforcing her life-long reputation for being outspoken and a little bit wild. Her father used to say, "I can either run the country, or I can attend to Alice, but I cannot possibly do both.

Many years later, my father met Alice again at a party in Washington, and she remembered him from her visits to Dayton. My father also recalled that there was often a great deal of animosity between the two Roosevelt families. Alice's side always felt they had a claim on the White House and the presidency that Franklin and Eleanor's side did not share. At one party my father attended, Alice once did an imitation of Eleanor to garner laughs, but he didn't find it the least bit funny. Dad thought the world of Eleanor, and never thought much of Alice's jokes, even though many people loved her caustic jibes. Dad found her attitude towards the president downright disrespectful. When referring to her cousin, she never used his title, and instead called him "Franklin." My father said that he had met her several times in his life, and that those times were more than enough.

MaryLouise had a different opinion of Alice Longworth. She met her at several parties during and after World War II, and my aunt also knew Alice from Northeast Harbor, Maine, a town where Alice came to visit friends and family and where MaryLouise settled eventually after the

Ray Bolger, who played the Scarecrow in the movie The Wizard of Oz, *often stayed at the Van Cleve Hotel. Bolger's legs were like rubber, moving and bouncing in every direction. Although he was very polite and friendly, he never let anything interfere with his daily workout, exercising for several hours every afternoon in the empty ballroom. Photo by Van Damm Studios.*

war. MaryLouise found her to be very funny, and generally liked her spirit. She told me that Alice very seldom went to church and that she believed in black magic, often casting a spell on a person with whom she was angry. I was surprised to hear this, but I think my aunt used to get a big kick out of telling me unusual and odd facts about people she had known throughout her life.

Both my father and my aunt told me that Alice loved to invite people known to hate each other to her dinner parties. She would seat them

next to one another, and if they didn't immediately get into an argument, she would see that they did by the end of the evening. Alice loved
controversy and was always more then willing to stir the pot.

A World Gone Mad

President Franklin D. Roosevelt (seated, left), Orville Wright (center) and former governor James M. Cox (right) at Wright Field in 1940. Courtesy of Special Collections and Archives, Wright State University Archives.

MaryLouise

My father's sister, MaryLouise, was always high spirited and adventurous, so it was probably inevitable that she became involved in the brewing troubles of the mid 20th century. Prior to and during World War II, she worked for the U.S. War Department, then transferred to army intelligence. She spent much of the late 1930s based in Madrid and traveling throughout Germany and other European locations, presumably assessing the deteriorating situation on behalf of the United States government. As a civilian who spoke German, and with German relatives, not to mention someone with extensive social contacts, she might learn things that official government representatives could not.

While many United States citizens of German ancestry faced discrimination during this era, I can only surmise that ours did not for the simple reason that by this time the family was well-to-do with powerful political friends. For years, former Governor James Cox saw the Breen family almost on a daily basis—first at the Phillips House and then at the Biltmore where he lunched regularly; he had known MaryLouise since she was a child. The Breen children were friends with Jim Cox, Jr. and his sister, Helen. Cox in turn was often visited by his old friend, Franklin D. Roosevelt, and long-time friend, Secretary of State Cordell Hull; the Breens were on friendly terms with all of them.

Cox was a newspaper publisher with his own interest in what was happening overseas, and he knew many of the generals stationed at Wright Field. Again, it's a guess, but it makes sense that this nexus could easily have led to a position of trust for MaryLouise, despite her German ancestry.

[This was not the case during World War I when the family's place in the national community was far less secure. At that time, they ceased communicating with Katherine's German relatives, using the German language at home, or serving German beers at the Phillips House, and so forth.]

MaryLouise traveled extensively throughout Europe beginning in 1935, and was in Berlin just one week before the German army invaded Poland in 1939. When Britain and France declared war on Germany, she escaped to Stockholm with the clothes on her back and seventeen cents in her pocket. She told the story thus in letters home that were reprinted in *The Sunday Journal-Herald*:

Panic of Americans Fleeing Germany
Seen by MaryLouise Breen in Berlin

Mary Louise Breen, a member of the special staff of The Sunday Journal-Herald, has spent the last month in Germany. Miss Breen, who has visited Europe many times in more peaceful days, gives an eye-witness account of Germany as it approached the fateful hour of war in the following two letters, dispatched by airmail from Stockholm just a few hours before the German forces invaded Poland.

Either I know very much less than you do, or very much more. There is absolutely no way of telling. The

DEPARTMENT OF STATE
WASHINGTON

June 14, 1937.

To the American

Diplomatic and Consular Officers.

Sirs:

At the instance of the Honorable
John J. Cochran, Representative in
the Congress of the United States from
the State of Missouri, I take pleasure
in introducing to you Miss Mary Louise
Breen of Dayton, Ohio, who is about
to proceed abroad.

I cordially bespeak for Miss Breen
such courtesies and assistance as you
may be able to render, consistently
with your official duties.

Very truly yours,

Cordell Hull

*Letter from Cordell Hull, United States Secretary of State,
requesting diplomatic consideration for MaryLouise, 1937.*

feeling here is that Hitler is beyond his depth this time
and that there is no way on earth of getting out of a
mess without war.

Getting home is something else again. The Kungsholm
is just a good break. The Queen Mary, with a capac-

ity of 2,000, has booked 4,000 for its sailing today and they are not sure she will sail. At Southampton, a tender full of passengers sailed around waiting for the Hansa—which never did show up and with no notice.

The real panic is on and it is quite something to see. If war starts, the Kungsholm has routed a course far to the north. So if she sails on Saturday with no change of schedule and I am on her I'll be home about the 11th.

Yesterday Swedish broadcasts urged the conservation of all supplies. There is an embargo on imported luxuries to conserve currency in the country. No gasoline allowed for pleasure trips. It is announced there is food enough for two years so no need to lay in supplies although everybody is doing it.

It's Exciting Game

Last Friday in Berlin was pretty exciting. I was with Jeff Patterson (first secretary of the American embassy at Berlin) at a gathering with British and American embassy and consulate members, newspapermen and steamship agents. It was a box seat at a pretty big game. Most of my prettiest tales are shot because people simply cannot be quoted. You cannot imagine or believe the discretion that must be exercised even in the simplest things.

The German border is closed now. The Czechoslovakian border was closed the whole time I was in Germany. One American consul with whom I was riding one day was scoffing slightly at the rigid instructions I had received on the care necessary in Germany. A little later we were talking about uniforms and I brought out of my purse a picture of a nice little Nazi I had met on the way -- "For God's sake, put that away. If they ever find that on you they'll stick him in a concentration camp as a spy." Which is typical.

I feel as if I have had a pretty extended bird walk on this trip and with luck I'll see you soon. My cheerios to the family. Tell them I am as safe as a church which is true.

Mary Louise Breen

Safe in Stockholm, Remembers Terror

How does it feel to hear a telephone ring in the middle of the night without floundering from sleep into instinctive panic and grabbing shoes and coat on the way to answer it? How does it feel to hear an airplane without wondering whether you are within striking distance of a bomb? How does it feel to go into a railroad station and not see mothers stroking the faces of half-grown boys in uniform, and fluttering handkerchiefs until the last arm has disappeared from a train window and then burst into tears? I have almost forgotten.

I have spent a month in Germany. I have seen tension beginning slowly and growing steadily day after day, increasing until now it pervades an entire nation and takes the form of an irresistible restlessness which is a perfectly dreadful feeling.

There has not been a single morning in the last two weeks when I have not been awakened by the sound of marching soldiers; the heavy rhythmical swing of thick boots; the disciplined full-throated marching songs; the rattle of artillery over cobblestone streets. There has not been even the smallest military detachment which has not had unusually large groups of spectators standing perfectly grave and silent, lifting their arms in the Nazi salute and turning away silently when the soldiers have passed. There is nothing gay in these parades. Sometimes they are the khaki uniforms of the party. Sometimes the black-garbed storm troopers with the red, white and black swastika armband. Sometimes the gray-green army uniforms with the dull steel helmets. Rumors spread like locusts and are repeated with a furtive secrecy. They go on and on, growing distorted, and only increase the general fear.

Speaks out of Turn

I was at breakfast one day in a private home with about 20 Germans of all ages. It was Sunday morning and the family had gathered after church. Because I was there as a guest, we had an extra supply of sausages and we had butter. The coffee was the usual "ersatz," a blackened grain which is completely without taste even in the kernel, and, boiled, has only the virtue of being hot. At the head of the table sat the grandmother who was old enough to be garrulous. I was obeying to the letter the rigid instructions which I had received when I entered Germany: "Don't ask any questions. Don't take any notes. Don't offer any opinions." The conversation was entirely general until the grandmother threw the table into a miniature panic by the very casual statement: "There will be war."

There was a moment of very embarrassed silence, followed by a chorus of concealing laughter and a few hush hushes. But of one thing we were all aware. She was voicing the definite opinion of everyone present.

That acceptance of the possibility of war was new and shocking to me. One person after another has told me confidently: "There will be no war. Our Fuehrer is too smart for that. We will achieve Danzig without a drop of blood being shed."

Little Information

The lack of information in the newspaper is appalling. For days on end England, France and the United States do not even seem to exist. There are front page stories of Polish atrocities and the inside pages of the paper are filled with accounts of the wine festivals and page after page of "help wanted." Unemployment simply does not exist.

There are exceedingly few American tourists and even before the real crisis there was an excited exodus. The consulates have registered all Americans and in the last week they have been besieged for information they do not possess. At this point Americans have been notified, and it is published daily, that unless there is urgent reason for staying all United States citizens should go home. Ships, planes, trains are packed. The German ships have been recalled and sailings cancelled. The United States ship I had planned to take from Hamburg sailed three days early from LeHavre without even calling at . . .

When the time came for me to leave, I bought a ticket to Stockholm and spent all my marks because I was not allowed to take any money out of Germany, and I arrived at the Berlin railroad station with two suit-

TELEGRAM RECEIVED

1 — 1143

From: M I L I D   Date: 24/12/43

                         No.:   409

Code: SECRET   Received: 24/12/43

PRIORITY   PRIORITY   PRIORITY

Following msg requires your urgent attention Quote For eyes only Milattache Amembassy Madrid. After reading CMIRI Winston and Joe want to meet Breen stop As your commander-in-chief I advise caution stop If in doubt send her to me not repeat not to Eleanor signed Franklin Unquote stop par The War Department naturally cannot comment but for your private information Breen can always find a desk with me stop You are urged to handle this matter with great discretion stop Reply immediately stop

STRONG

For Miss Breen:

Please reply by indorsement giving full explanation of what you have been up to.

Wm. D. H.

One of many telegrams MaryLouise received
regarding her war activities based in Madrid.

cases, an extra hat in hand, a bundle of papers, a piece of chocolate, and a total capital of 17 cents. The train was bulging with returning Swedes, and my feeling of being an isolated immigrant disappeared in the mass of paper suitcases, bundles, baskets, packages, screaming children and assorted dogs. There was simply no room for me. I plunged into the milling mass of the next train and sat. It did not seem to make much difference to me at the moment that I had a Swedish ticket, the enormous sum of 17 cents, and that I was on a train bound for Norway.

Borrows and Bribes

In the next compartment a weeping Scandinavian was telling the conductor that she had no money and there was a fury of conversation before she disappeared into the limbo of third class. The trainmen and the guards had long and serious conversation over me. It ended when they all scratched their heads and shrugged their shoulders, and then I knew I had won by out-sitting them. I ended by borrowing four marks from the conductor and bribing him with them. On the ferry leaving the German border I was switched to the Stockholm sleeper—if sleeper it could be called. It has all the aspects of a cattle train in its more crowded moments.

From here, getting for the first time in a month a broader international picture I still have a complete sense of unreality. I wake up in the night hearing the tramp of soldier's boots and the rattle of cannon carriages. I can see women controlling their faces. I can see half-grown boys with pink baby faces marching off so proudly and so solemnly in their uniforms. And I can see statesmen filled with greed and lust and pompous words seeing how close they can hold their lighted tapers to the smoldering volcano without setting the world on fire.

Mary Louise Breen

[Author note: When the *Journal-Herald* folded in the 1970s, the Cox chain purchased that paper's archives and rights; many photos from the *Journal-Herald* appear throughout this book.]

According to my father and others close to MaryLouise, she more than likely was with the Office Of Strategic Services (O.S.S.)—the precursor to today's CIA. MaryLouise was associated with the American embassy in Madrid, and her reputed mission was to enter occupied France disguised as a nun, find downed Allied pilots, and smuggle them safely back into neutral Spain. A telegram dated December 24, 1943 with references to "Winston" (Churchill?) "Joe" (Stalin?), "Eleanor" (Roosevelt?) and "Franklin" (Roosevelt?) has always intrigued the family, especially given the main author (General George Strong, head of Army Intelligence) and the note at the bottom to MaryLouise.

*Captain Breen, pictured on far right, is shown here participating in
gas mask training with fellow soldiers. United States Army Photo.*

Additional support for our suspicions that she had been in the O.S.S.
is provided by the fact that many of her friends, who also lived on Mount
Desert Island, including Julia Child, were known members of O.S.S.

Her wartime letters to my grandmother were frequently very vague,
and although I've always felt my aunt had as many stories to tell as my
father did, unfortunately she rarely shared them.

Eddie

On December 7, 1941, my father was sitting in the lobby of the Van
Cleve when a desk clerk announced, "Mr. Breen, the Japs just bombed
Pearl Harbor." My father didn't believe him—he thought Pearl Harbor
was too heavily fortified. An hour later, though, my father, a captain
in the National Guard (he was an ROTC member in high school and
joined the Guard after returning from Cambridge), received a phone
call from his commanding officer giving him just enough time to say
goodbye to his mother before reporting for active duty. Knowing he

would not return to Dayton for a very long time, if at all, he resigned his position as manager of the Van Cleve.

By the time he and four other men from the Dayton area arrived at their duty station in Kentucky, they learned their unit had pulled out seven hours earlier, headed for San Antonio, Texas. My father ordered a pair of military policeman standing nearby with their motorcycles to escort his Jeep until he could rejoin his unit. When the younger man said, "I can't go sir, because I'm getting married in a week," my father told him in no uncertain terms, "You're in the army now. You have one hour to get your girl up here and get married." An hour later, the M. P. was married and my father was off to catch up with his unit somewhere on the road to Texas.

Upon arriving, they were greeted with a large headline in the local newspaper that said in big bold print, TEXAS DECLARES WAR ON JAPAN AND GERMANY, and in much smaller print, "The United States also declares war on Japan and Germany." A little-known fact about Texas is that when it joined the Union in 1845, it reserved the right to declare war separately from the rest of the United States.

After a brief stay in San Antonio, my father's unit was to be stationed at Fort Bliss in El Paso, guarding the American border in the event that Mexico should invade Texas.

Duties at Fort Bliss were taken seriously, but there were times when a few hours away from the base provided a much-needed chance to relax. One night, my father and two of his fellow soldiers went to dinner with three young women from town. Afterwards, my father casually remarked that his date had a wooden arm. His friends didn't believe him so he bet them $20.00 that he was telling the truth. A few evenings later, they went out again with the same young women. Back at the base, each of his friends silently handed him a twenty dollar bill. A year later, when they arrived in North Africa, my father and his two friends were sent to different locations. On Christmas Day, Dad received a fancily-wrapped package with an unsigned card attached. Inside was the wooden arm of a department store mannequin holding a bouquet of wilted flowers. His fellow soldiers never understood why my father burst out laughing.

Before going overseas, their unit was sent to Wisconsin for further training. The wet cranberry bogs in the dead of winter were cold and uncomfortable, and no one knew where they would eventually be sent,

On board troopship

Dear Mother, John , Mary Louise, Ad, Beckey , Johnny, and Mrs Gilbert :

So far so good, and we have had a ______ of sailing around

more the merrier.

Life aboard a ______ can be put in one sentence "it aint no pleasure cruise" however its not one half as bad as I actually expected it to be. I am assigned to a state-room which in the good old days was

place looks like

figure it out)

This is not exactly a lazy life for just about the time you get comfortably streched out in a bunk you can expect to hear

you have a chance to get in a first class yawn.

There are ______ served ____ and the entire personnel is served within two hours which is an excellent record for thorough planning and organization on the part of some one.

Every day at twelve o'clock noon there is a fifteen minute religious service and if you are interested you go with your team, and Chaplain Sullivan holds his rally on the Port Side, Sunday was our troopship sodality day and there were hundreds of Catholics going to

Letters home were often less than informative for the recipients as they often arrived with large chunks cut out, thanks to army censorship. This one was written on the troopship from the U. S. to North Africa.

although rumors floated that they were going to help defend the Soviet Union from Germany. After weeks of intense conditioning, the unit finally boarded a train whose windows had been painted over. The Army Corps of Engineers had also changed many of the billboards along the tracks. For example, a sign that read, "Welcome to Lincoln, Nebraska," might have been in Toledo, Ohio. This was done to confuse any spies who may have been among the troops.

En route, the men were given warm gloves, boots, coats, and thermal underwear; they felt it more and more likely they were going to the Russian front. Their troop train traveled to Fort Dix, New Jersey, and the soldiers transferred directly from the train to the ships, with guards lining their path to ensure the men did not talk to civilians.

MaryLouise visited my father before he boarded his troop ship. Due to her contacts, she was able to enter the staging area and give him a gift—a small, sterling silver box containing a set of dice for good luck. He attached them to his dog tags so they would always be with him. Whether or not the two made a conscious and mutual decision, they both took pains throughout the war to keep letters home upbeat so as not to upset their easily alarmed mother. My father went so far as to have his dog tags engraved to indicate that his sister should be notified in the event of his death or serious injury, rather than his mother.

On his first night at sea, my father was so far below deck he could hear German submarines moving beneath the ship and the Navy dropping depth charges to try to destroy them. Ever prepared, the men slept fully clothed and wore life jackets. After several days at sea, their heavy gloves, coats, and long underwear were taken away and they were instead issued short sleeved shirts, short pants and desert-brown boots. Best of all, they were finally allowed to go on deck for a breath of fresh air. When my father looked across the water, he realized they were flanked by hundreds of other Navy vessels. Only then did he realize the enormity of the operation of which he was a part.

North Africa

By November of 1942, my father's infantry unit was ready to enter the war. The troops assembled on deck to hear a speech by General George Patton, commander of the Western Task Force, who was on the convoy's flagship, the U.S.S. *Augusta*. Patton explained that they had been zigzagging off the coast of Africa for several days, and that the next morning they would be landing near Casablanca, on the western coast of North Africa. They were a part of "Operation Torch," in which the Western Task Force was to invade French Morocco from the Atlantic. Patton expressed his confidence in the American troops, saying he knew that every soldier would do his job.

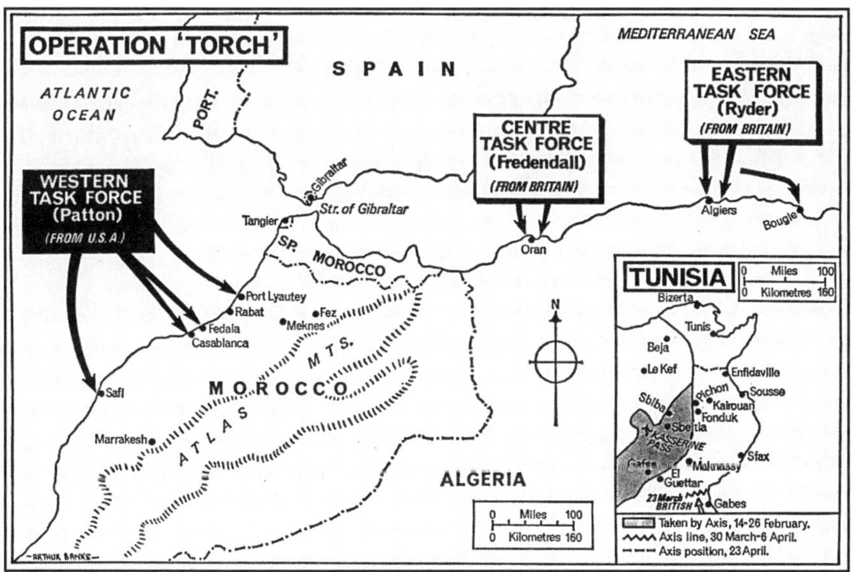

Operation Torch was my father's introduction to World War II combat. Sketch by Arthur Banks from the West Point Historical Atlas. *United States Army Map.*

After Patton finished, an officer stood up before all the men and asked if there were any questions about the general's speech. One soldier's hand shot up and he asked, "In his speech, the general said the fighting would be 'in tents.' I would just like to know what kind of tent—pup tents, wall tents, or dome tents?" The comment lessened much of the anxiety and fear, at least for the moment.

The next morning, November 8, 1942, the task force received the order to "play ball". Bombers from the U.S.S. *Ranger* attacked Casablanca harbor followed soon after by the U.S.S. *Massachusetts* firing her massive, sixteen-inch guns. Nearby battleships soon followed suit. The landing parties split into thirds with the objective of surrounding and taking Casablanca. My father's infantry unit landed at Fedala with General Patton's Central Group, slightly to the north of Casablanca.

The fighting wasn't half as bad as the soldiers had expected, and more than one man jokingly said, "When the Germans heard the Americans were coming, they turned tail and ran." Many of the men didn't understand that they weren't fighting elite German troops, but rather the Vichy French. There were many French officers who were less than committed to the alliance with Germany and surrendered after minimal resistance. Others, while furious with the British (who had recently bombed French naval vessels to keep them out of German hands), were uneasy about fighting against the United States with whom France had enjoyed a long friendship. The resulting invasion was hardly a cakewalk, but nothing compared to what the Americans would soon experience.

§

The Allies in North Africa dealt with the complicated relationship between France and Britain in a variety of ways, including sometimes putting British troops under U.S. command and in American uniforms. In turn, U.S. troops wore American flags displayed prominently on their sleeves to distinguish themselves from the British. There were also tensions between the British and the Americans, ranging from rivalry, to resentment by the British that the Americans had waited so long to enter the war.

Troops had a way of settling matters directly, as my father soon witnessed in a Casablanca restaurant packed with British and U.S. troops. A G.I. sitting at the bar absentmindedly rubbed a British coin back and forth across the bar, perhaps as a deliberate provocation, perhaps not. In any event, a British solider asked him to stop rubbing King George's face in the beer suds. When the American indicated that he would be happy to turn the coin over and instead rub the king's *ass* in said suds, a brawl erupted. Incidents such as these were common.

§

In February 1943, the newly trained American troops led by General Lloyd Fredenhall (commander of the Centre Task Force) entered Kasserine Pass in Tunisia, where they were severely beaten by the German air force and Rommel's elite tank corp. My father actually served under Patton, but he and several other officers were constantly on the move negotiating with Arab chieftains, and he found himself attached to the Kasserine debacle almost by accident.

There was utter panic as the pinned down troops tried to escape that narrow pass. My father's Jeep was following a truck full of Gurkha soldiers from Nepal who were part of the British Eighth Army. The Gurkhas were known as fierce warriors and presented a terrifying mien, going into battle in bare feet and with teeth filed into fine points. They each carried a *kukri*, a razor sharp, sixteen-inch curved knife thrown like an Australian boomerang and used with pinpoint accuracy. A joke told among the Allied troops was, "After having a *kukri* thrown at him,

THE WHITE HOUSE

WASHINGTON

Capt. Edward G Breen

THE WHITE HOUSE
WASHINGTON

TO MEMBERS OF THE UNITED STATES ARMY EXPEDITIONARY
FORCES:

You are a soldier of the United States Army.

You have embarked for distant places where the war is being fought.

Upon the outcome depends the freedom of your lives: the freedom of the lives of those you love—your fellow-citizens—your people.

Never were the enemies of freedom more tyrannical, more arrogant, more brutal.

Yours is a God-fearing, proud, courageous people, which, throughout its history, has put its freedom under God before all other purposes.

We who stay at home have our duties to perform—duties owed in many parts to you. You will be supported by the whole force and power of this Nation. The victory you win will be a victory of all the people—common to them all.

You bear with you the hope, the confidence, the gratitude and the prayers of your family, your fellow-citizens, and your President—

Franklin D Roosevelt

Letter placed on each soldier's berth before the North Africa invasion and after General Patton's speech from the deck of the U. S. S. Augusta.

Following letter received from Ed Monday Jan 4th, 1943.

December 14th, 1942.

Dear Gang:

Just because I'm lazier than the average Breen I think if I tear a few pages out of the pamphlet which was issued to the men while on board ship that it will tell the story of this country much better than I would make an attempt to write about it ..... ah! the ingenious Breen. (He had enclosed a small booklet on North and Northwest Africa,it described our British and French Allies, Geography, Morocca, Algeria, Tunisia, Hygiene, Insect bourne diseases, Native populations, Moslem Religion, Attitude toward women and Important do's and Don'ts & I8m sending it to Mom as I presume you got one in Washington)

We are located in a wonderful spot, interesting as the duece, and every minute is packed with some new and interesting scene. Yesterday (Sunday) the native Colonials (French Foreign Legion) sent their drum and bugle corps and band to serenade us, they have about a fifty piece outfit and are twice as good as any American Legion drum and bugle corps you have ever heard or seen. These boys were dressed in powder blue jackets with white belts and white gloves, white turban headdress, scarlet pantaloons with gold braid and jet black wrapped leggins and shoes and looked like Mrs. John Vanderbilt Astor.

We are slowly but surely getting out of bivouac (pup tents) and I believe that within a day or so all of the men will be quartered in barracks. The French are cooperating by moving their troops to other locations in the vicinity and allowing us to share the artillery and infantry barracks which will make an ideal setup for a permenent camp site for American troops. Most of the officers have found rooms in private homes or in the hotel and little Sonny Boy is staying with the Colonel and the staff at the French General's home as his person guests. Our schedule for the day is about as follows; up at 6 and drive down to camp with Col Phillips, Capt Don Bering and Capt Naylor and have breakfast with the troops after a few hours work at headquarters we meet the French Staff, usually about 10 A.M. and then its salute and shake hands and go round and round in finding out how each other is after which we salute shake hands and then go into the second round of the discussion, in the middle of which we all stand salute, shake hands and to make it more official, salute again. The hand shakes and salute coming at frequent intervals but somehow usually catch me by surprise and I find myself jumping and saluting and shaking hands just a wee bit behind the others, but after all they set a pretty fast pace and its hard for an amateur like me to keep up.

Everyone is in fine spirits and today our Christmas Party Committee was formed to make plans for a nice dinner, or at least a surprise like instead of eating C or K rations, we will eat B rations which is a simple matter of re-issuing a different tin can. All joking aside we are eating very good food and there is not a kick from anyone. The food we serve here at every meal would be a real banquet to the French civilian or Military for after all they have been under some pretty tough food rationing for a couple of years. Our B rations are arriving now and that means we will have plenty of potatoes, eggs, milk, jams, ham, bacon and other meats. And we are planning on ~~smoking~~ throwing a real dinner for the French Staff real soon and I know they will enjoy the food we have available to offer.

Blackouts here are the real thing and the entire town is swallowed up by the darkness shortly after the sun sinks behind the mountain range and then you grab your coat because its colder than a refrigerator in a matter of minutes.

Johnny would get a big kick out of seeing the native soldiers. I do. They are really picturesque and should be done in oil painting as they are the most colorful and impressive figures you could ever possibly hope to see. And their horses would make the ones in Ringling Brother's circus take a back seat... gosh they are superb ... both horses and riders. The soldier is a sleek lookinf individual with a hawk like eyes and a well trimmed beard, his head is wrapped in a turban and he wears flowing robes and carries a t remendous rifle slung over his shoulder and an interesting curve knife, from the looks of things he would be a tough customer to meet as an enemy. However they have been courteous and we are busy all day exchanging salutes. Most of these native soldies are Riffs and come from this section of Morocco.

Letter written by Eddie Breen from North Africa the month after the invasion.

a German soldier told the Ghurka soldier, 'you missed me,' and the Gurkha replied, 'you think so? Try nodding your head.'" Allied troops were almost as afraid of the Gurkhas as the Germans were, and hated standing guard duty with them at night. As the truck full of Gurkhas tried to outrun the machine gun fire from German airplanes overhead,

Captain Breen shown here leading his fellow soldiers in a victory march in front of captured Vichy French headquarters at Casablanca. The defeated French are to the left in the photo. United States Army Photo.

they missed a curve in the road and plunged over a steep cliff, killing them all. The helpless screams of these brave men as they dropped to their death bothered my father for years.

Ultimately, over 1,800 men died and hundreds more were taken prisoner. General Eisenhower and General Patton were shaken by the huge loss of men and equipment at Kasscrine; Eisenhower replaced General Fredenhall with Patton who brought much needed organization and structure to the North African operation.

After many tumultuous months of reorganizing troops and acquiring replacement equipment from the United States, my father's unit was finally organized into groups of three Jeeps each called "rat patrols" that went out at night looking for German truck convoys traveling through the desert. Each Jeep carried a machine gunner who sat in the back, a driver, and a man in the passenger seat who carried a hand-held machine gun. One night, my father's team crested a small hill and he got out to scan the horizon, seeing something moving in the distance. Because it was dark, he assumed it was a German truck convoy and he got back in the Jeep to speed after the mysterious object. Suddenly, they slammed into something, flipped over, and all the men were thrown out. There was a loud shriek and lots of screaming and fast movement. My father fired his submachine gun, which only added to the confusion. Finally, everything was quiet.

As it turned out, his group had slammed into a camel caravan loaded with straw. When the Jeep flipped, the machine gunner was thrown into the side of a camel and had pieces of straw embedded in his face, arms and legs. He was the one who had uttered the loud shriek, and the other unidentified screaming and movement had come from the camel drivers. The machine gunner was taken to a field hospital immediately and, fortunately, recovered.

§

While in Rabat, Morocco, General George Patton was invited by Sultan Muhammad V to review the Moroccan military. It was a grand celebration with lots of fancy military uniforms and a large Moroccan military band to accompany the soldiers. Soon after, my father received orders from Patton's headquarters to take two men with him and deliver two U.S. military Jeeps to the sultan's palace as gifts for his young sons.

The three men drove the Jeeps and stayed to teach the sons (Prince Hassan II, successor to his father on the throne, and Prince Abdallah) how to drive. My father was awed by the beauty of the palace and surrounding grounds. After the driving lessons, he and his fellow soldiers were invited into the palace for a lavish dinner party. Their table was laden with elegant Moroccan food, and they ate an absolutely delicious meal of couscous with lamb and vegetables, accompanied by mint tea poured from a solid gold pitcher into sterling silver goblets. For dessert, several types of almond pastries were served.

As they ate, women dressed in native garb performed traditional folk dances and sang Moroccan folk songs. To my father's ear, the songs had a great deal of Spanish influence, or perhaps it was the other way around. Afterwards, several of the sultan's guards performed a sword dance—the most elaborate the Americans had ever seen. After the dinner and show, one of the guards presented my father with a sword and silver scabbard, into which were carved Moroccan military insignias. My father had the sword sent home, and it remains in my family.

The exquisite sword was not the only gift my father received while in North Africa. Earlier that year, he accompanied several other officers and an interpreter to a meeting with a group of nomadic Tuareg chieftains. American troop trains were being attacked in the desert by Arab men riding camels and horses, and my father hoped to convince the chieftains to allow the trains safe passage. As at the sultan's palace, my father and his entourage were treated as honored guests. They sat

Scenes from North Africa during my father's time there with Operation Torch. While they found them exotic, soldiers in North Africa (including my father) disliked camels because of their ill-temper. United States Army Photos.

May 30TH
Sunday
Rec'd in July '43

Dear Mother :—

Just came back from mass at the cathedral and the place was just jammed with American soldiers and sailors (dogfaces and gobs) — There were so many Americans there that arrangements were made to have a navy chaplain on land to read the gospel and give a short sermon in English following the French Arch-bishops sermon.

Sending you a couple of old brong and copper trays — they are not too special — and they need to be polished a bit. — They were given to me by the French families that I visited at my last station.

Watching a funeral yesterday and believe me they do a pretty fancy job of it — black carriage with silver trimmings — black plumes on horses heads, black uniformed

Eddie Breen's letter to his mother.

on fine, handwoven carpets inside a large tent and were served a meal of *pastilla*—a heavily spiced pie of lamb, pigeon, and vegetables. As the highest ranking officer, my father was offered the lamb's eye to eat. All of the officers were given gifts, and my father received a small, unusual-looking cross known as a Tuareg cross, which he strung on his dog tags alongside the dice from MaryLouise. Among the Tuareg people these driver who sits high up on the wagon and holds in his white gloved hand an impressive looking whip which he can crack with a noise almost sufficient to awaken the dead. — Everyone walks in rows following the hearse — and the success or failure of the affair depends strictly on the size of the parade,

An Arab funeral is another story and I'll wait until we meet to go into that — its necessary to have the proper sound effects — and believe me they can chant in grand style. The story the GI's are telling this week is one about the two sardines awaiting a jeep to be transferred to another camp. — after waiting for quite some time one sardine suggested they forget about the jeep and go by troop train. The other sardine said, "What and get packed in like

The cut-off last line at the bottom of this attempt at soldier humor reads: "What and get packed in like soldiers?"

crosses are passed down from father to son, and are meant to be symbols of protection. Several times, my father told his mother that just before the front of the landing craft came down during invasions, he would reach under his shirt and pull out the cross and dice, kissing each for good luck.

Dad and his friends found the Moroccans to be extremely generous and gracious hosts, leaving them with nothing but kind thoughts and warm feelings.

Even though its people were generally friendly, the desert was anything but benign. Once, late at night, a guard heard a noise on the roof of the barracks. He called out, "Halt! Who goes there?" but the noise continued. Believing a German sniper was on the roof, my father was awakened by his troops and was outside in a matter of minutes. After the guard called out again and received no response, the guard fired a warning shot. Again, they heard the noise. Finally, he fired his rifle in the direction of the noise and a loud thud was heard seconds later. When they went to inspect, they found the source of the noise—a very large leopard on the ground, now dead. A large group had gathered to see what the commotion was about, and when they saw the animal, they all wanted to have their picture taken with it.

Despite the hardships, Dad loved being in both the military and North Africa. He often said it was like living a scene from *Beau Geste*, the desert adventure story he loved as a child.

One day, my father received a call that one of his men had been killed at a forward outpost that happened to be a private residence. Accompanied by his driver, a doctor, and another soldier, they drove into the desert to recover the soldier's body. Several hours later, they found the home and parked the Jeep at a safe distance. None of them wanted to be the one to knock on the door in case it was a trap. The four sat in the Jeep and argued among themselves until a young native girl yelled down from the roof, "What are you silly boys doing down there?"

At that, they all went to the door. The owner of the home invited them inside and once again they were treated to an elaborate dinner party complete with dancing. The next day, they returned to camp with the soldier's body. To explain the extra time they had been away, the men pretended that they had been lost for hours.

My father met his dear friend, Albert Stern, in North Africa shortly after the invasion. When the draft board asked Albert for his pre-military occupation, he wrote "movie star", thinking perhaps he would get sent to California to make propaganda films rather than shipped overseas. It didn't work, but his "occupation" remained in his military records from then on.

Soldiers surround leopard which was shot to death when the men heard late-night noises and mistakenly thought it was a German sniper on the roof. United States Army Photo.

Lieutenant Stern was generally disliked by the other officers, and often the subject of ridicule. Unlike many of the officers, he had never been a Boy Scout, gone to West Point, served in the National Guard, or had any other military connection. His uniforms were invariably sloppy, he called enlisted men by their first names, wouldn't read manuals or learn procedure. By his own admission, he "didn't know and didn't care." In addition, he was one of the few Jewish soldiers in the group, further isolating him. Stern was also a "ninety day wonder"—drafted as a private, but due to a shortage of officers he had been trained in ninety days and promoted to the rank of lieutenant. Before his military duty, Stern lived with his mother in a high-rise in Champaign, Illinois. He had never so much as played toy soldier as a child (in fact, it was forbidden), and his only goal while overseas was to stay alive long enough to return home to his mama. Lonely, terrified, and miserable, Albert had taken to drinking until he met my father, who promised that he would personally ensure Albert's safe return.

Perhaps as someone who was himself very close to his own mother and sister, my father could empathize, or maybe he just took pity on the man, seven years his junior. Whatever the reasons, the two men became nearly inseparable, in spite of repeated warnings to my father from his fellow officers who were convinced that Stern was totally unreliable and could not be counted on in difficult situations.

Albert told me years later that "God had better things for your father to do than die in war," so he figured if he stuck close by, he too would survive. It worked.

§

One of the sadder aspects of life as a wartime officer was the duty of writing to the parents of the men in the unit who were killed in action. It was always a heart wrenching and difficult experience, especially if the officer had known the soldier well. When my father had to perform the task, he would sit and stare at his typewriter late into the night, at a loss for words. When inspiration finally came, he wrote letters full of compassion and sorrow. As he recalled later, "In my mind I could always picture my own mother reading such a letter, and I always hoped that it would be written by someone who cared about her feelings."

Even more difficult to write were the letters that declared a man missing in action, especially when it was all but certain that the man had died in combat. Such was the case later in Bari, Italy. A good friend and fellow officer was on the docks when an intense German air attack on the harbor began. The next day, soldiers found the man's boot with a part of his leg inside and his dog tags nearby. Still, the military would not declare him officially dead because not enough of the body was found. My father said anyone who lived through that night in Bari would know there was not a chance the man had survived, but the military required that he write to the man's parents and simply say that their son was missing. Thinking it cruel to send the parents false hope, he tried to phrase the letter in a way that would let them know their son, in all likelihood, was dead.

Once, very late at night, air raid sirens sounded while my father was visiting a friend at a field hospital. German planes could soon be heard overhead, and the ground began to shake from the nearby explosions. The lights in the field hospital flickered and finally went out. The helpless, wounded soldiers began to scream in terror. Brave doctors and nurses went from bed to bed in an effort to reassure their patients, even

Captain Breen. United States Army Photo.

though the hospital staff no doubt feared for their own lives as well. As my father recalled years later, "You just felt so helpless and prayed the bombs would not fall anywhere near the hospital."

My father's one bit of normalcy overseas were the letters that he received from his mother and his brother, John. Katherine wrote three or four times a week and John, who was now married, wrote nearly as often. John's two children, Johnnie and Becky, were a source of great pride to my father. They were his only nephew and niece, and it gave him great pleasure to hear about their lives back home. He collected military emblems from the various armies with which he came into contact and sent them to Johnnie. In many ways, focusing on his niece and nephew took away the harsh reality of the war.

My father rarely received letters from MaryLouise, who was also overseas and as involved with the war as he was. However, MaryLouise

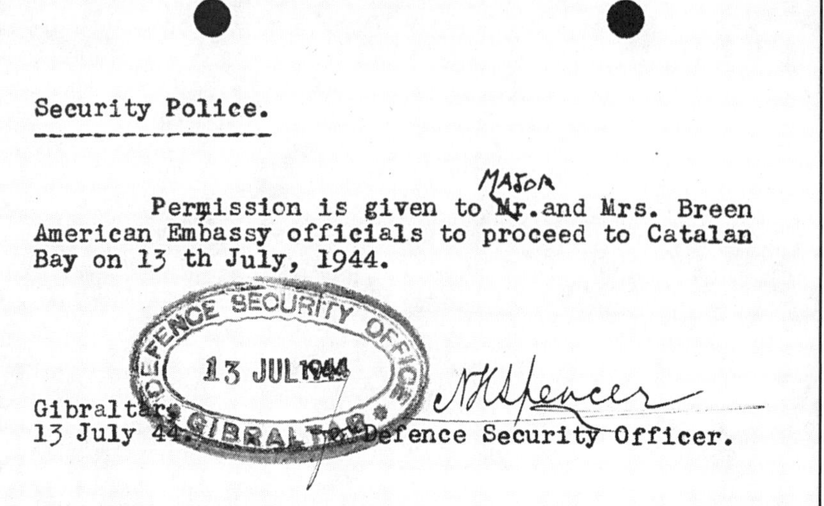

Security pass issued to MaryLouise Breen allowing her to enter Gibraltar on July 13, 1944. Whether a mistake or done for security reasons, she and her brother are named as "Major and Mrs. Breen."

was able to stay informed of my father's location. Often she knew where my father's unit would be sent even before he did. Once, he received a letter from her that said, "When I see you in two weeks on Gibraltar we will have a grand reunion, love your sister, MaryLouise." Army intelligence censors read the letter, and were immediately suspicious. They told my father that since Gibraltar was a British fort and women were forbidden there, they did not believe that his sister had been the one to write the letter. When he insisted that he was telling the truth, the officers said they would investigate. However, army intelligence never contacted him again, and two weeks later, MaryLouise was at the Rock Hotel in Gibraltar as planned. According to MaryLouise, although it had been built only a decade before, "the hotel looked to be about 100 years old, as dilapidated as an old barn, and four times as dirty." She reported that my father was in awe of the setting—British officers sitting alone at tables, reading quietly in their spotlessly clean khaki or white shorts, oblivious to the less than perfect wartime conditions. As instructed by his superiors, Dad delivered a lead-sealed leather pouch to MaryLouise when he arrived. She never revealed what was inside the pouch, but my father recalled that it was labeled "not to be searched by customs officers."

These men were about to be shipped to prisoner of war camps in the U.S. from the port of Algiers. Because of his native fluency in German, Captain Breen often interviewed German prisoners of war captured in North Africa. United States Army Photo.

MaryLouise wrote years later that as she and my father sat on a balcony of their hotel that night, they heard an air raid siren. Soon, they saw the silhouette of a German airplane caught in the powerful beams of the British searchlights. When MaryLouise heard the British anti-aircraft guns, she prayed silently for the German pilot who was about to lose his life. It bothered her that her brother continued sitting calmly, showing no reaction. Finally, she asked him, "Doesn't this upset you?"

His only reply was to say that he saw this occur every night in North Africa and Italy. Describing the evening years later, MaryLouise wrote, "I can see how this war changed the two of us forever."

Before my father left for war, his mother gave him several gold coins and told him to use them to contact his German relatives if he was taken prisoner. She knew that some of the cousins were in the German army and she thought her son might meet them at some point, perhaps not considering that if they did meet, it would be as enemies. Since my father spoke fluent German, he would often be sent to the docks in Algiers to speak with the German prisoners before they were sent to American prison camps. His mission was to gather any relevant intelligence information. Knowing that his mother was concerned for her German relatives, he would also ask if anyone knew the Beckman family. Later in the war, he learned from one of the prisoners that his cousins Johannes and Joseph had been taken prisoner and sent to the United States, and that their younger brother, Alois, and their father had been killed in action in Belgium in 1940. Upon hearing this, my father burst out crying. He told me years later how surprised he was at his emotional response, particularly considering the violence and carnage he had witnessed firsthand. Perhaps it was the memory of seeing his cousins as children when he and MaryLouise visited them in the 1920s.

Prisoner of War

Upon learning his cousins' fate, my father wrote to his mother. Katherine eventually discovered that a prisoner by the name of Hans Gefreiter Johannes Beckmann of Wallenhorst, Germany was at Fort Custer, a prisoner of war camp in Michigan. My grandmother wanted to visit, but because she was a civilian the army would not allow it. It's not entirely clear in which order the first three letters were received in spite of the dates, as they all underwent military processing.

USA, 01-01-1945

Dear Aunt,

Because some days ago I received your address through a letter from home, I want to send you some greetings. You will be surprised to receive a letter from a prisoner of war in America. My name is Johannes Beckmann from Wallenhorst, near Osnabrück. I come from the farm from where your father once migrated here. Fate brought me in June here to America and exiled me behind barbed wire. At the present time I am at the German prisoner of war camp at Fort Custer in Michigan. Because in the beginning I unfortunately did not have your address, but often heard from my father that you live in America, I often asked for the name Beckmann in vain until I received your address from Mr. Hartlage from Osnabrück. You will also be happy to hear something from a relative, and I would like to hear from you.

Greetings to you, your Johannes Beckmann

[Author's note: the German spelling is Beckmann.]

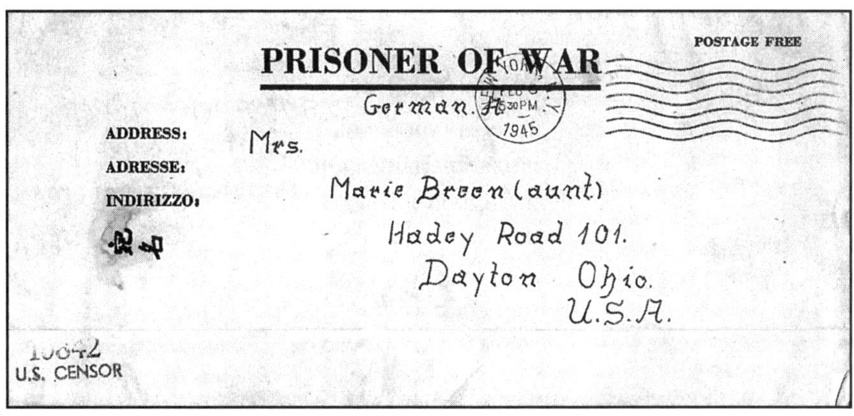

Envelope containing letter sent to Katherine Beckman Breen by a relative held as a German prisoner of war at Fort Custer, Michigan.

An old family friend, Major Joseph E. Keller, undertook to locate Beckmann and wrote this on January 27, 1945 (not a relative, he always addressed my grandmother as "Aunt"):

Dear Aunt Kitty and Eddie:

I now have the following information about Hans:

Gefreiter Johannes Beckmann, Serial No. 81G-247904, born July 4, 1924, home—Wallenhorst near Osnabrück.

He is at the prisoner of war camp at Fort Custer, Michigan which is near Battle Creek. Under the prisoner of war rules, he can be visited by mother, father, grandmother, grandfather, uncle, aunt, wife, children, brother or sister.

If you will address a letter to the Commanding Officer at Fort Custer, Michigan, he will send you the rules for sending packages and food, as well as mail for him. I believe if Eddie explained the circumstances to the Commanding Officer that he would probably be glad to allow Eddie to visit him.

I hope this is all the information you will need, but if you want any more, let me know and I'll also be glad to find out what you hear after you write to Fort Custer.

With kindest regards,

Cordially,

Joe

Rules were rules, however, and it was not to be as the request was denied in a letter dated February 7, 1945.

Still, Johannes was luckier than many, returning home healthy and safe at the end of the war. The Breens received this letter written from Wallenhorst and dated September 22, 1946:

Dear relatives:

Perhaps it is unknown to you why I needed to suddenly discontinue writing to you. However, I hope that you rejoice with me and my family that I now can send you cordial greetings and a thank you from my home in Wallenhorst.

Very often my thoughts were with you and my comrades who had to stay back, who perhaps to date await their fate while behind the gruesome barbed wire. I cannot forget the time when I too was fenced in by the barbed wire and from where I sent my greetings with the wind to my far away homeland from which we were cut off for an unknown time.

Thus from home to yours I would like to send you, my dear relatives, best regards with the same inner sentiments and with my abundant thanks. I hope this letter finds you in good health. I assume that you have quite often wondered about me how I could be so ungrateful to you by never responding by letter to you. But, no, I cannot even express in words how happy I was to have found a piece of home away from home. But my joy was not supposed to last long. I had received one letter and two beautiful packages while I was in the infirmary in McAllester [Oklahoma]. In January I had been transferred there from Camp Custer in Michigan.

The second package with the beautiful Easter cake, Easter eggs and cigarettes arrived here long before Easter and it contributed much to my Easter happiness. My thank you letter for this package was not meant to reach you any more. Fourteen days after I had mailed it, it was returned to me with the remark 'cousin.' The American commandant of the camp forbade according to the treaty that I may continue to write to you. I told them that you were my aunt; thereupon the letter was mailed again but likewise returned. What could I do? Everything else was in vain if I did not want to expose myself to punishment. Thus, unfortunately, my joy found a quick end insofar as I was not able to thank you in writing before my trip

```
                    ARMY SERVICE FORCES
                    Sixth Service Command
          Headquarters, Fort Custer, Michigan          SSS/mw


                                            1611 SCU PW Camp
                                            7 February 1945


SUBJECT:  Request to Visit PW Johann Beckman, Gefr, 81G 247904

TO     :  Major E. G. BREEN, AC, 101 Hadley Road, Dayton, Ohio

     1.  Unable to grant permission to visit PW Hans Beckmann, Gefr,
81G 247904.

     2.  Provost Marshal General rules that only the closest blood
relatives may be permitted to visit Prisoners of War.  Cousins are
not in that category.

     3.  PW's are permitted to receive any amount of mail, or pack-
ages, subject to censorship.

     4.  Correspondence between yourself and PW Beckman will usually
take considerable time enroute.  The delay is due to the time mail
is held by the District Postal Censor, New York City.

          For the Commanding Officer:



                                STANLEY S. SWANSON
                                1st Lt.,    AUS
                          Security & Intelligence Officer
```

Letter response to Eddie Breen's request to visit Johannes Beckmann.

home for all your endeavor and work to ease the helpless lot of my captivity. This settlement was an embarrassment for me.

Shortly after Easter I had surgery (hernia) which went well. About four weeks into my convalescence we were informed that the entire camp would be dissolved and all the inform were discharged. Fortunately, I had the great luck to be among the first 1400 to be allowed to go home. From the port in Charleston we spent 12 days on board of Aleda de Lux to Chesburg. From there we continued to Munich from where I was officially discharged on August 25. At first I could not believe to be free again, liberated from the barbed wire which for so long had kept us captive. On August 28 I arrived at home. In their first shock my dear relatives cried and laughed to express their joy. Fortunately, they had preserved from the war so that everything is alright here. My oldest brother Joseph returned also from his captivity. Now we are all together and at home with the exception of my younger brother Alois who died in action in Belgium in 1940. My father dies also in 1940.

The four of us live now on the farm: my mother, my sister Theresa, my brother Reinhold and myself. I enclose a small picture of our farm for you and I hope you are happy about it. Much has changed since you had been here.

Likewise in Osnabrück it looks dreadful. One can only see ruins when one walks through the beautiful old streets of the city. Life here has much declined especially since so many refugees from the East have come. Food is scarce but we hope that it will be a little better after the coming harvest. At home we cannot complain; we are all healthy and everything is like in the good old times.

Now I think that this letter has reached its due length. Therefore I want to conclude. Once more I would like to express my most cordial gratitude to you for your generosity granted to me with a "May God reward you!"

With cordial greetings from my mother, my sister as well as my brother, I remain with much gratitude yours,

Johannes Beckmann/Bechmann

SICILY

In July 1943, American forces invaded Sicily. My father's unit, part of the Seventh Army commanded by General Patton, participated in the invasion, code-named "Operation Husky." Amphibious vessels had evolved in the six months since the invasion of North Africa and could now ground directly on the beach and lower a bow ramp so that men and matériel could disembark closer to shore. Known officially as Landing Ship, Tanks or LSTs, the men not so affectionately called them "large, slow targets" and "lousy, stinking tubs." It took Allied troops thirty-eight days to conquer Sicily, and the success of their mission triggered the fall of Mussolini's government. It was an important win for the Allied forces.

In the late summer of 1943, General Patton was relieved of command for slapping two soldiers hospitalized for battle fatigue. Several months

Johannes Beckmann, 1943. He was taken prisoner at the Battle of Anzio in Italy on May 23, 1944 and sent to various prisoner of war camps in the United States until the end of the conflict. Courtesy Johannes Beckmann, Jr.

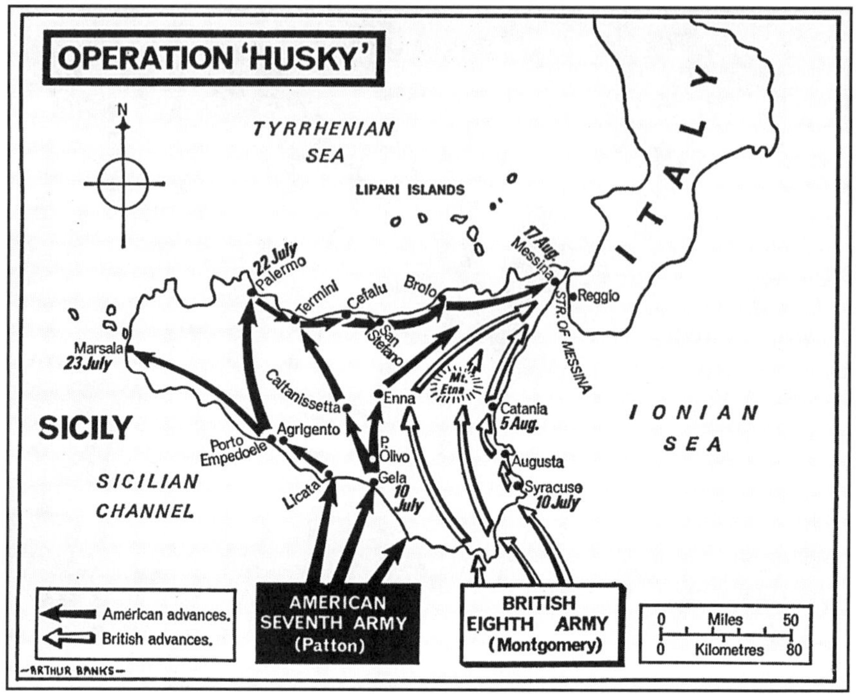

Drawn by Arthur Banks for the West Point Historical Atlas of World War II. *United States Army Map.*

later, Patton was sent to Britain to command the newly formed Third Army, and was replaced in the Mediterranean by General Mark Clark. For the most part, the soldiers were happy about the change in command, as Clark was considered to be less arrogant and brash. My father, however, did miss Patton's drive and dedication.

While in Sicily, my father often flew back to Algiers, North Africa with the other officers for debriefings. On these trips, their plane was always escorted by the 99th Pursuit Squadron, which was made up of the famous pilots trained at the Tuskegee Institute. These airmen were the first African American pilots to serve in the American Armed Forces, and they compiled an impressive record in both North Africa and Sicily. They gained such an excellent reputation, in fact, that many of the officers refused to be escorted by anyone else. My father always said that he felt more secure on these trips when he could look out the window of his plane and see the 99th's trademark red tail section.

During his service, my father knew several of the Tuskegee Airmen, the first black pilots to serve in the American Armed Forces. Unfortunately, my father did not record the names of the men in this photo. United States Army Photo.

MAINLAND ITALY AND OPERATION AVALANCHE

Naples

After landing in Sicily, the Allied forces moved on to the Italian mainland. For my father, this was the roughest invasion of the war. His one comfort was the knowledge that he could count on the men around him.

Prior to invasions, the troops would climb over the side of the large Navy ships via cargo nets down into the much smaller personal landing craft (LCVP—Landing Craft Vehicle Personnel). This already dangerous climb, particularly in rough seas, was made more difficult by the large backpack and rifle the soldiers carried. Each boat transported 32 men, all loaded the same way. The three men carrying dynamite were always put into the rear of the boats, and in front of them would be two medics and a member of the clergy, if one were available. Next would be a three-man team carrying flame throwers, and in front of them would be two mortar teams of three men each, and then two men with a bazooka and two men to carry the shells for the bazookas.

Then came two teams of riflemen, and in front of them would be three soldiers called "BAR men" because they carried a hip-firing Browning automatic rifle (BAR) that could fire a .30 caliber slug at 650 rounds a minute. This is where my father was stationed in the boat. In front of him was a three-man team with heavy wire cutters designed to cut the barbed wire on the beaches. Finally, in the very front, there was a junior grade officer with a .45-caliber pistol. Each man was equipped with five grenades and four smoke grenades, and the BAR men carried an extra 900 rounds of ammunition.

The ten-mile trip from the ships to the beachheads, during which the men had time to think about what lay ahead, was frightening. The LCVPs were difficult to maneuver and often their flat bows would dip into the waves, soaking the men with spray. Many soldiers bailed water with their helmets. As they neared the beaches, the Germans would begin firing and the men would try to keep their heads as low as they possibly could. Many soldiers broke down at this point, crying in fear.

Once the front end of the LCVP came down, all hell broke loose. My father frequently told the younger soldiers to grab onto a buddy as they waded ashore, but once they reached land, it was every man for himself.

Dad told me that he felt closest to God in those minutes after pushing off the mother ship and starting the LCVP's diesel engines. (Years later, during our summers in Maine, the sounds of the lobster boats reminded him of the distinct, high-pitched sound of those engines.) In the first few minutes on the open sea, some soldiers would tell jokes or make wisecracks, but as soon as the vehicles got within two miles of the beaches, and bullets from the German machine guns began pinging against the sides of the LCVPs, the men would become deathly silent. A few recited the Lord's Prayer or the Hail Mary. He said at those times one or two soldiers would ask him in a low, sincere whisper, "How do you pray to God?"

On the morning of September 9, 1943, they bounced across the turbulent water in an LCVP as hundreds of Allied warships floated off the Italian coast to provide backup for the incoming assault, code-named "Operation Avalanche." At 4:30 a.m., several of the larger battleships opened up with their large deck guns, creating a thunderous roar as they shot missiles toward the German defenses fifteen miles away. As they headed toward the beaches near Salerno, hundreds of airplanes

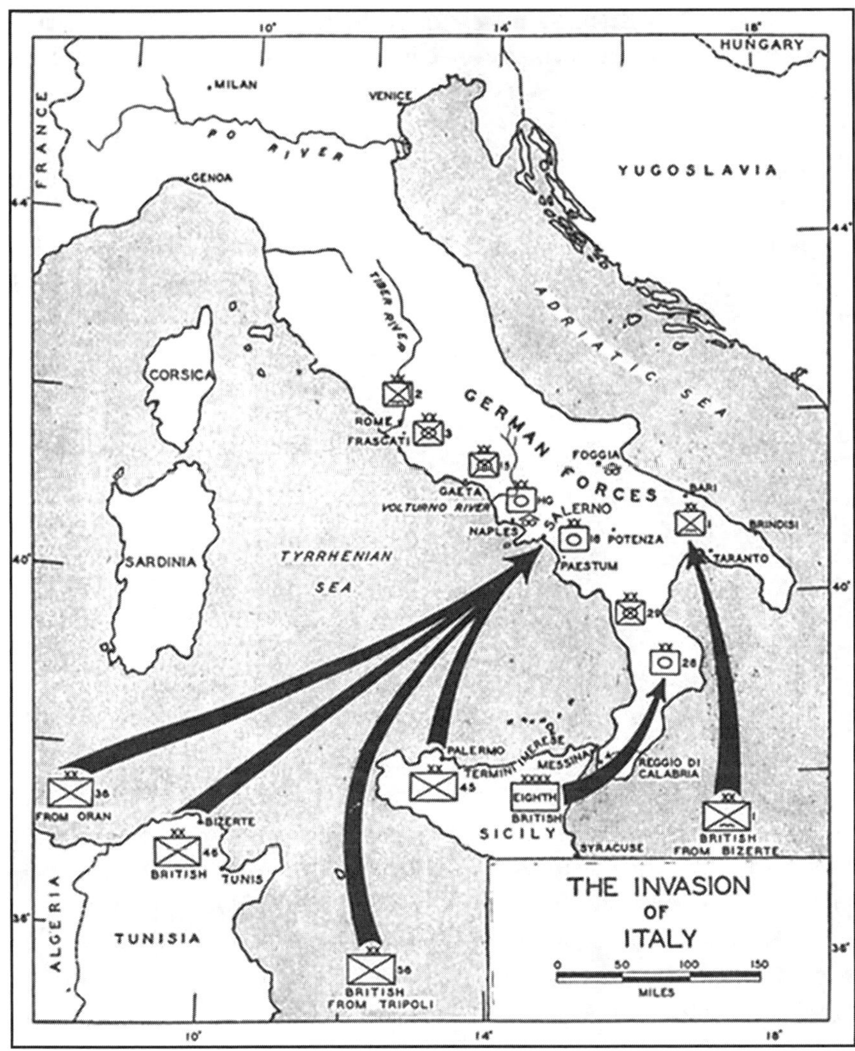

Invasion plan. United States Army Map.

stretched across the morning sky bringing in the paratroopers of the elite 82nd Airborne Division.

Upon landing, it was utter chaos. Before the invasion, my father had been given a map of their landing area. He'd studied it carefully and felt confident that he would know where he was. However, the reeds and grasses had caught fire, creating so much smoke that the map was useless. At the same time, the ground below the soldiers' feet was shaking like an earthquake from all the explosions. Incoming mortar rounds from the German defenses ruthlessly ripped off heads, arms, and legs while they all felt intense heat from the flame throwers wielded by men crouched a few feet away. His only thought was to survive the nightmare.

Both in the North African and Italian invasions, many soldiers drowned in the ocean. Some didn't know how to swim and when they left the LCVP boats they would step into crater holes created by the bombs. Because of the heavy equipment they carried, they would slip underwater and not resurface. The soldiers had been instructed to pull a lever on the front of the pack to release it in such a situation, but often they would panic, forget, and, subsequently, be lost.

Others were shot or killed even before they had a chance to leave the landing boats. German troops raked the beachheads with a heavy concentration of machine gun fire, mowing the soldiers down like ducks in an arcade game; the horror of it could never really be described. It was a world gone mad and anyone who survived the carnage of an invasion was forever changed.

On mainland Italy, the Allied forces faced stiff German resistance. My father's unit fought its way up the Amalfi coast before reaching Naples on October 1. Dad felt the real heroes in the invasion of Italy were the Corps of Army Engineers, who worked a day ahead of the troops, removing rubble from the roads and rebuilding bridges that the Germans had destroyed. Practically overnight, the engineers could reconstruct a bridge strong enough to hold the weight of a tank.

Once they reached Naples, destruction and disease were so widespread that only troops who had been properly inoculated could enter the city. The German army had left Naples just the day before the Allies arrived. Before their retreat, they had blown up buildings, cut phone lines, and left rubble blocking the streets. They had also taken street cars, taxi cabs, and any other spare metal they could find and dumped it all into the harbor in order to make the port unusable to Allied ships. The German army had shot horses, cows, chickens, and other livestock, then dumped their carcasses to contaminate the freshwater sources. Residents and soldiers alike were left with very little food and no drinkable water. Worst of all, the Germans left all sorts of inventive booby traps—light bulbs filled with gasoline that burst into flames when power was restored, phones rigged with explosives, and even posters of pinup girls set to detonate if a G.I. tried to remove them from a wall.

King of Italy Victor Emmanuel III is the elderly man in the middle of the photo. The car behind him is the limousine that he later gave to my father. United States Army Photo.

On that day my father was in his Jeep leading an infantry column of about 600 men in trucks supported by several tanks into the battered city, when he passed two elderly men standing beside the road. Next to the men was a beat-up limousine that had obviously been a very elegant car at one time. The two men flagged them down, and identified themselves as Victor Emmanuel III, the King of Italy, and Barone Oreste Ricciardi. The Barone told my father that if he would promise each of them a truckload of food for their families, they would guide the American forces into the center of Naples. My father agreed, and thus began his long friendship with the two Italian noblemen.

My father and the other officers took over the former central post office as their command headquarters. Unbeknownst to them, one wall in my father's office was false, and behind it was a charge of concealed dynamite set on a timer. On October 7, several days after setting up headquarters, the men in my father's office drew straws to see who would walk the three blocks to the rolling canteens to pick up lunch. Dad and three other men drew the short straws. As they were returning with their food, the dynamite exploded, destroying the building and

Barone Oreste Ricciardi signed this photo dated April 1944:
"With the bad things the war brought me something good—your
dear friendship. Sincerely, Your new old friend . . . April 1944"

U. S. troops searching for the dead in Naples. United States Army Photo.

killing many of the men inside. In all, over 100 people were killed that day, many of them civilian women and children who happened to be passing by at the time. My father and the three men with him were slammed into a brick wall from the force of the explosion. They lost many friends thanks to that explosion, and if they hadn't drawn the short straws, they would have died as well.

Italian troops searching for the dead in Naples. United States Army Photo.

Later, my father's unit moved outside of the city. For reasons he never explained, the beat-up limo was given to him as a present. It fit in quite nicely with the large villa that he and his fellow officers shared in the countryside.

As time passed, Dad's friend Albert Stern began to show signs of battle fatigue and the men grew increasingly worried about him. One day, a priest arrived at their door, saying that he would bless their home for a donation. Although Jewish, Albert gave him money and then proceeded to have the priest bless everything in the villa. The more he blessed, the more Albert gave. Albert had the priest bless the bed he slept in, the chair he sat in, and the porch he relaxed on each morning. The priest left a much wealthier man—and Albert felt much safer.

Another soldier living at the villa had informally adopted an orphaned eleven-year old Italian boy. The boy was paid a little money to do odd jobs and was given bits and pieces of old uniforms to wear. He even had his own bedroom in the villa. None of the men spoke Italian and could not pronounce his name. As such, they all took to calling the boy "Willie." Willie liked to talk a lot, and when the men got tired of

Major Breen saved fruit and rations for the children caught up in war, as did many others. United States Army Photo.

his constant unintelligible jabbering, they would say, "Oh, piss on you, Willie." One day, a gruff-looking army nurse approached my father on the street and asked, "Captain, can I talk with you about Willie? He came to me a few days ago and said that you and your men are always saying 'Oh, pizzona, Willie.' He has no idea what you're trying to say. He loves living with you and only wants to please. If it's something that you'd like for dinner he would be glad to make it. If you tell me what

'Oh, pizzona' means, then I can explain it to him." My father was terribly embarrassed, and told her that he thought it was a type of French bread. He promised to have one of his men bring her a sample, and with that, he hurried off. He always avoided the nurse after that.

Many of the U.S. soldiers felt a fondness for the children caught up in the war. My father often took the cigarettes that came with his meal and traded them for the apples which also came with the meal package, giving them to the children he encountered as he walked about town. As an officer, he also had the option of choosing canvas or leather seats in his Jeep. He always picked leather, and he recalled years later how he would wake up some mornings and find the seats in his Jeep stripped bare. Fellow officers would ask him why he never posted a guard. But my father knew that the children who cut the leather from his seats needed it for shoes.

One morning, Dad woke up after a particularly heavy German air attack and stepped out onto the villa's balcony to watch the sun rise over the ocean. He joined Albert, who was already there with a cup of coffee. Immediately, my father noticed something Albert hadn't—a bomb from the night before had landed and wedged between the iron railings that surrounded the balcony. Completely unaware, Albert was reclining with his feet propped on it. My father turned white as a ghost as Albert bid him an oblivious, cheerful hello. Not wanting his friend to panic, he said very calmly, "Al, please don't move. Your feet are resting on a bomb." The coffee in Al's hand began to tremble, but he listened to my father and didn't shift a muscle. My father got the other men out of the building and called for the soldiers trained in bomb disposal. They were able to defuse the bomb, and once the threat was over, Al was endlessly teased. Certainly, the incident must have worsened his already frayed nerves.

Bari

After staying in Naples until mid-November, 1943, my father and some of his troops left for Bari on the eastern (Adriatic) coast to pick up supplies for the American forces that they were unable to get through their own port at Naples. (The port at Naples was open by this time, but security was tighter in Bari and felt to be safer for bringing in dangerous supplies such as mustard gas.) Before they could collect the supplies, German bombers attacked the harbor on December 2, destroying 17 Allied freight ships in one of the most dreadful nights of the war.

The enlisted men's billet in Naples after it was bombed in 1943. Officers operated from the old Main Post Office building nearby; my father was alone in his billet during the raid, and it, too, was severely damaged even though it didn't sustain a direct hit. United States Army Photo.

*Captain Breen before the attack on
Bari. Photo United States Army Photo.*

Frank Fisher, a United Press staff correspondent, described the raid in a clipping my father saved:

London, Jan.20 - German bombers flew over Bari Harbor at 10,000 feet on the night of Dec. 2 and blasted it into a hellish nightmare of exploding shells, leaping flames, and shattered buildings by a lucky hit on an ammunition ship. I stood under the clear star-lit sky on the opposite side of

*A postcard shows the opulent Miramare Hotel in Bari,
Italy as it appeared before it was bombed. My father and
other officers were billeted here during the Bari raid.*

the harbor from the target docks and watched the sight
in all its terrific magnificence. The harbor was jammed
with ships. The planes announced themselves with a string
of flares which lighted the harbor. The bombs came down
without warning. There was a terrific explosion. The whole
sky seemed to fill with a dull reddish flame. A sailor near
me whispered, "My God, they got the ammunition ship."
There were a few seconds of silence. Then a wind whipped
through town like a tornado. There was a continuous
crunch of breaking glass, punctuated by the heavier sound
of doors, window frames, and Venetian blinds being ripped
out. We could only conjecture the havoc wrought amidst
the ships and personnel. (U.S. Secretary of War Stimson
announced on December 16 that there were roughly 1,000
casualties to service personnel.) Scores were wounded by
flying glass. They walked about as if stunned. A naval officer, who was slightly wounded in the blast, told me later
he stood within 200 yards of the ammunition ship when
it went up and was not even knocked down. Yet ten miles
inland, the wind from the blast blew out windows. The
ammunition ship set afire other nearby ships. Some sank
swiftly and some burned all night. I counted nine ships
partly sunk or burning so fierily they could not be saved.

Anyone who witnessed the bombing of Bari Harbor on December 2, 1943 never forgot it. Shown are three of the 17 ships that exploded in the harbor; they are seen here still burning three days later. United States Army Photo.

In a February, 1952 letter describing my father's wartime service, former Staff Sergeant Harry Radezky described the night of the Bari raid:

Following the first enemy air strike, Capt. Breen immediately proceeded to Headquarters at the Miramare Hotel but en route was caught by a full force of one of the explosions from an ammunition ship. All blasts from the 17 ammunition ships were terrific in violence and all personnel and civilians in the vicinity of several miles were dazed and stunned by the heavy blow.

That evening I first saw Capt. Breen as he entered the Miramare Hotel (a four story building used as officers' and enlisted men's mess and advanced squadron headquarters). Capt. Breen proceeded to his room to secure his helmet, gas mask and tommy gun and 45 Colt automatic pistol and had left orders through Sergeant Esce to round up all available enlisted personnel and to report immediately combat-equipped and without pack.

*My father's office at the Miramare Hotel after
the bombing. United States Army Photo.*

*During the next few minutes, two terrific explosions took place
ripping out the corner of the four-story building and blasting
windows out and tearing down a great amount of plaster. Breen
along with others shared in a deluge of plaster and flying glass. He
had taken cover during this time in his room with Medical Officer,
Capt. Tirey. Following this blast Breen posted a guard detail around
the building with orders to challenge everyone and to be especially
alert for civilian saboteurs and enemy paratroopers.*

*In a Jeep which I drove for Capt. Breen, we proceeded to the
Finance Office and posted a guard there. Sergeant Esce and I
accompanied the Captain to make a quick survey of the situation
in the harbor and dock area and during this time we were forced to
take protection from another series of blasts by lying in the gutter of
the street to shield us from the concussions, flying glass and debris.
We also checked a XII AFSC installation along the bay to see if there
were any officer fatalities. A bomb had exploded along side of this
installation . . .*

Air raid shelter at Bari, Italy. United States Army Photo.

Later at the Miramare Hotel another officer's meeting was held and it was learned that one unexploded ship was filled with mustard gas and was in immediate danger of explosion. Also, there were certain British Units in the area which had already been evacuated to a point ten miles from the city. Capt. Breen was ordered to organize the evacuation of all troops of our command who were not by necessity required in the city. (Security for Bari was under the British Eighth Army.) Breen's orders were also to include all Americans. This was done under the most adverse circumstances imaginable. Rubble blocked the traffic on most streets and there was a general hysteria among the Italian civilian population which were in the process of evacuating the city. The evacuation was hampered by the collapse of several large buildings and by the general confusion of the population.

Former captain and medical doctor James Tirey also recalled:

I could not attempt to describe the horribleness of that night of Dec. 2nd at Bari. It defies description and would put the story of Dante's Inferno on a rear shelf. Each individual participant I feel sure carries many unpleasant memories that not even time will erase and I feel

Destroyed airfield at Bari, Italy. United States Army Photo.

sure too that an "X" amount of physical damage occurred to all participants of the Bari raid, and I know as I speak for myself.

At least one of the ships that was hit contained mustard gas which leaked into the atmosphere. Doctors speculated years later that at least some of my father's health problems stemmed from exposure to the gas at this time.

For several days before the attack, my father and some of his officers had noticed a red light on the roof of a building, which was odd as the town was under blackout restrictions. They drove into town each day and night trying to locate the building, but failed to do so in the maze of city streets. On the night of the raid, my father was standing on the balcony of his villa with two roommates, two or three miles distant from town. The men watched the first wave of German planes fly over and drop low-falling chandelier flares. These flares lit up the harbor as bright as day—with his binoculars my father could see people walking by the docks. The next wave of planes quickly followed, dropping red target flares. The third wave dropped the bombs. From his vantage point, my father realized that all the planes were lined up with the red light they had seen in previous days.

Many American airplanes were destroyed by hot ashes from the eruption of Mount Vesuvius during March, 1944. United States Army Photo.

Even at a distance of several miles, the wind from the explosions was strong enough to lift my father off his feet. He was thrown through a plate glass window and slammed into a wall so hard that he was knocked unconscious; his heavy wool officer's coat saved him from being sliced to death by flying shards of glass.

Dad was always surprised that Bari had been hit so hard, as he thought they were well-prepared for any attack. The British used giant fogging machines to shroud the harbor, and the Army Corps of Engineers had built a fake cardboard city many miles away that they lit up at night to fool the German planes. The fake city and the fog made navigation quite difficult from the air, which was why the Germans had used a red light to coordinate their attack. The day after the air raids, my father had his men fan out across the city in an intensive search for the light. A few days later they found it, shielded on a roof. It was immediately destroyed.

Major Breen and the Ferneding Twins

After Bari, and once he arrived back at Naples, Eddie Breen was promoted to the rank of major.

Major Breen (pictured on far right) with fellow soldiers outside an air raid shelter in Naples, Italy on April 16, 1944. United States Army Photo.

Several of my father's friends took the war-torn limo given to him by King Victor Emmanuel III to an Army repair yard. There, they fixed it up with spare parts, even adding flags to the front wheel covers. Just as he had back in Texas, my father struck a deal with two motorcycle MPs, and he allowed them to live at the villa in exchange for escorting him around town. The limo looked very official and was a big hit with all the men. But after nearly seven months in Naples, his unit received orders to move toward Rome.

My father couldn't bring the limo, but he settled on a solution after receiving a letter from his cousin, John Ferneding (John's father, Henry, was the judge Protestants railed against in the anti-Catholic pamphlet years earlier). John served in the Navy and his ship was scheduled to arrive in Naples the day after my father's unit pulled out. The morning that John's ship docked, the big car with siren-blaring motorcycle escorts came roaring down the pier, looking so official that the sailors all thought someone famous was coming to visit the ship's captain. The commotion caused every man on board to line up on deck. As they peered down over the side, a very fat Italian woman stepped from the limo and placed a call from the shore phone to the ship. Soon, the ship's intercom blared for Lieutenant John Ferneding to report immediately to the bridge. John arrived at the bridge to find the ship's captain glaring at him. "There's a woman down there asking for you. What's this all about?"

With the captain still glaring, my father's puzzled cousin answered the phone, whereupon the woman announced, "My name is Ava and this limo used to belong to your cousin Eddie. His unit pulled out yesterday, and he's giving you this limo, the motorcycle escorts, and a villa up in the hillside with a fully stocked wine cellar." John shared his good fortune with his fellow sailors, but he never invited the captain to use the house or the limo because the man was so grumpy.

John and his twin brother, Tom, had their own rather amazing tale to tell from their war service. They were assigned to separate ships upon entering the navy to ensure a better survival rate, something the military preferred to do when siblings enlisted. Tom served in the Pacific Theater and John was sent to the Atlantic. In August of 1942, John was transferred to the Pacific Theater and the U.S.S. *President Jackson*, a transport ship charged with bringing in troops and supplies, and evacuating casualties. The brothers had lost track of each other's whereabouts by this time, and had no idea that they were both on ships engaged in the battle for Guadalcanal. Tom was on board the heavy cruiser U.S.S. *Astoria* during the Battle of Savo Island just off Guadalcanal. The *Astoria* was sunk on August 9, 1942 after sustaining severe damage during a blistering Japanese night action and the *President Jackson* was ordered to pick up survivors. A sailor woke John to tell him that they had just pulled a man from the sea who was a dead ringer for him and he raced to the deck to find his badly wounded twin. As Tom lay on the stern deck waiting medical care, John gave him a crucifix and rosary beads, saying, "Let's pray to God that you make it, Tom." A photographer on the ship happened to get a photo of the moment, and it went out over the wire services, where the photo and story were picked up by Dan Ryan, a reporter for the *Universe Bulletin*, a Catholic newspaper in Cleveland, Ohio. Tom and John both survived the war, with Tom marrying the Navy nurse who cared for him while he recovered. Ironically, Dan Ryan somehow met John after the war, and went on to introduce him to his sister, Ada, whom John married. The entire unlikely story was written up in *Reader's Digest* a few years later in the 1950s. Meanwhile, though, there was a war still on, and John went back to the Atlantic Theater where Eddie's surprise awaited him

John (left) and Tom Ferneding circa 1945.

Endgame

After leaving Naples, my father and his fellow soldiers discovered just how perilous traveling in Italy could be. As they retreated, the Germans had switched or torn down many of the road signs, replacing some with false names. His unit was bombed continuously as they came up the hill to the old abbey at Monte Cassino; he developed frostbite and lost feeling in his hand, although others obviously suffered far worse. In the end, the troops were defeated by a combination of the mountains, the winter, and the Germans. It was not the American troops, but rather members of the Polish army (Poland had been liberated by the Soviet Union) who ultimately took Monte Cassino and cleared the way to Rome.

One evening while in Rome, Dad and three friends decided to have dinner at Alfredo's, a world famous restaurant. Looking in the windows, they could see the place was packed with American and British officers. Alfredo himself told them he had no tables and to come back another night. Turning to leave, my father remembered something he had read in a magazine, and casually said to the man, "Next time you see Mary Pickford, tell her I said 'hello.'" At that, Alfredo lit up like a Christmas tree. "You know Mary Pickford?" (Alfredo's was her favorite Roman restaurant). With a straight face my father answered, "I most certainly do," although in truth, he most certainly did not. Alfredo responded, "Any friend of hers is a friend of mine. Come back in, I have one table I keep on reserve for her. You can have that special table tonight and I will serve you personally. You will be treated like royalty." With that, he ushered the men inside. The other officers stared as Alfredo served them one of his best wines and personally mixed their salad with a spoon and fork given to him by Mary Pickford and Douglas Fairbanks. He fussed over them all evening, and when they left, he refused payment, saying, "When you get back to the States, tell Mary how I treated you." They reassured him that the very next time they saw her, they would.

A few days later, while walking around the Vatican, my father and his friends saw several British officers in dress uniforms waiting in line to see the Pope. Even though they were in unwashed battle fatigues, they joined the queue. Eventually, two Swiss guards ushered them all inside. They marched down a long hallway and into a small room. Soon the Pope appeared, walked up to each one of them, and gave him a blessing. Before moving on, he asked each person a few questions. After blessing my father, he asked where he was from. Since my father had heard that the Pope had once been to Cincinnati, he said, "I'm from Cincinnati." The pontiff answered, "That's nice," in a low, quiet voice, and continued. When they were back outside, Albert said, "I thought you were from Dayton." Dad answered, "I am." "Then," Al replied, "that makes you the first person I've ever heard of who lied to the Pope."

Although Rome provided the American soldiers with some desperately needed lightheartedness, my father, along with Albert Stern and many others, was showing signs of battle fatigue. Two major incidents occurred near the end of their stay in Naples that ultimately led to their return to the United States—Albert after a few months in Rome, and my father a few months later.

One night, Albert, Dad, and two fellow officers finished a quiet dinner in one of the few restaurants still open in Naples. Walking home, the four of them decided to take a side street. Suddenly, two shots rang out and instantly killed the two men in front. My father instinctively jumped into a doorway and flattened himself against the frame as bullets continued to fly. Albert, meanwhile, had dropped into the middle of the street, kicking his legs, waving his arms, and screaming, "Oh my God, I don't want to die!" From the doorway, my father yelled, "Albert, roll to the side of the street. Albert, roll now!

A U. S. serviceman receiving baptism on the grounds of Caserta Palace, 25 miles north of Naples. The twelve hundred room palace was headquarters to Generals Mark Clark and Harold Alexander. United States Army Photo.

Do it, for God sake! Roll to the side of the street!" In a state of panic, Albert simply could not hear him. Having observed where the shots were coming from, my father stepped out into the street and opened up with a burst of gunfire from his Browning automatic rifle, killing both snipers. He then grabbed Albert, and half-pulled, half-dragged him to the curb. According to Albert, the burst of gunfire coming from the Browning rifle was the sweetest sound he would ever hear if he lived to be a hundred. After regaining their composure, the two made it back to their quarters, where they called a medical unit to give the location of the bodies. The assault had a profound effect on both men, and it was something from which neither fully recovered. My father only mentioned it once or twice in his later life.

The second incident occurred soon after, and from what both men later told me, it was the final straw. Dad, Albert, and the sergeant who drove my father's Jeep were near the dock area of Naples doing a late night inspection when the air raid sirens sounded. Within a short time German bombs cascaded down. Seeking shelter, the sergeant drove away

Major Breen in Italy. United States Army Photo.

from the harbor and back into the city area. A building collapsed in front of them, blocking the street, and when they tried to turn around, they discovered more debris blocking the street from behind. The three left the Jeep and began to run, climbing over rubble as they went. As they turned down another darkened street, my father saw what he thought was a dead baby lying on the sidewalk, and Albert saw what he

Major Breen (far right) and fellow soldiers surround a captured German machine gun in Italy. United States Army Photo.

thought was a second dead baby. Since they were within several blocks of a hospital, my father suggested they take the bodies to the hospital to receive a proper burial. It wasn't until both men had picked up the bundles and a nearby explosion brightened the night sky that they discovered they were holding not dead babies, but rather two halves of a woman. Albert held the head and my father the lower half of the body. As both men began to go into a state of shock, Albert said, "You know ol' Breeno, every time something like this happens to us, you always end up with the good parts." Even though Albert was able to make a joke, the macabre incident shook them to the core. Several days later, my father put in a request to have Albert sent back to the United States. It was not granted for another eight months, but Albert finally returned to the States, where he was hospitalized and underwent shock therapy for battle fatigue.

Several years later, Albert Stern entered the construction business in Champaign, Illinois and became a wealthy man; he named the first street of homes that he finished "Breen Drive." He insisted that my father come to Champaign for the dedication, where Dad finally met the colorful Mamma Stern, about whom he had heard so much. She was a delightful woman, everything that Albert had said and more.

Twenty-five years later, Albert had retired and moved to Long Boat Key, Florida. When my parents visited him, at every restaurant, art gallery, gift shop, and harbor club, Albert introduced my father as, "Lieutenant Colonel Edward Breen, the man who saved my life." My father always found it embarrassing, but he loved Albert like his own brother, and their bond remained strong until Albert died in July of 1986. [Author note: My father was promoted to Lieutenant Colonel in the Infantry Reserve when he was released from active duty.]

According to my father's staff sergeant, Harry Radezky, Dad's deteriorating mental state was also the primary factor determining his wartime return to the United States. In his 1952 letter supporting my father's desire to seek medical assistance from the Veterans' Administration, Radezky wrote:

> I regret that I was not particularly alert insofar as suspicioning [sic] Capt. Breen had suffered a shock more severe than perhaps we realized. However, upon recalling events I remember that from about that period of time on his absence from Officers' mess was noticeable and many officers inquired as to where he was, although not too much thought was given for everyone knew that the Captain also made a practice of eating with the troops in the enlisted men's chow lines. But, as I recall now he was conspicuous by his absence even there during the last month or two of his overseas assignment.

> I know that Breen for the last few weeks or months had been suffering from occasional attacks of dysentery accompanied by chills. (I believe this trouble began from Bari where upon arrival, there was no running water and bad sanitary conditions due to the fact that the Germans damaged the water system before evacuating the city.)

> Major Breen complained to me during the last month or two that he had not been sleeping any too well at nights and I now recall that during the last month or few weeks before Breen's departure, he went into an almost complete "shell" insofar as any great association with members of the command, which was certainly contrary to his past makeup. However, on the many times

that I was with the Major he often remarked that he was finding it difficult to "shakeoff" the bombing that I have mentioned in the preceding paragraphs and that for the first time in his life he was finding eating not a pleasure.

I was in a Jeep with the Major several months after the particular bombing just mentioned and at this time, he saw Capt. Maurice Bradford, Aid [sic] to Brig. General Harold Barton, Commanding General of the XII AFSC and in the curbstone conversation that followed, Breen advised Capt. Bradford that he planned to initiate a request for his return to the United States and asked the Captain's help in speeding this request, listing two reasons: One, was that he did not want to serve under a new general, and Second, he told Capt. Bradford that he had been feeling "rocky" and had the "GI's" (dysentery) and thought it best if he could get back for a short period of rest.

Perhaps what could be listed as significant is an affair that took place at Capt. Breen's billet around 6:30 in the morning, the day that Sergeant Esce, Corp. Corbin, Private Simms and I called to assist the Major in getting to the airport for shipment to the States.

Breen was in a state of complete emotional breakdown. His packing had not been finished; he was unshaven and he seemed to have lost all sense of coordination and also complete loss of control of his emotions. Breen looked as though he had not slept during the night and that perhaps, he had been crying for several hours. He was crying at the time we arrived and continued this emotional upset even to the departure time to the airport.

This was also absolutely contrary to his usual calm and collectiveness and cheerfulness that he had displayed during the many months of our association.

Our first thought on seeing the condition of Mr. Breen was that he had been celebrating his return home but there was not any evidence of any wine or liquor and we were soon positively convinced that he had not been drinking (although, at the time, he gave the enlisted men several unopened bottles of wine which he had obtained in Gibraltar). There was no reason for us to jump to the above conclusion inasmuch as we had never seen the Major under the influence of intoxicants at any time during his service with the Command.

The emotional outburst was so out of line and contrary to his past performances in North Africa, Sicily, and for the year in Italy that it was a topic of conversation and discussion among us for the following weeks. We believed at the time that he was merely upset on leaving his friends in the Command.

. . .I believe that he was ill then and I believe now that he was ill when he departed from Naples and I am firmly convinced that his illness resulted from some of the experiences of his two years' overseas service.

I share the opinion of all enlisted men and officers of the XII AFSC Command that he was an excellent Officer and a fine gentleman and it was a pleasure to have served under his Command as advanced Headquarters Commandant of the XII AFSC.

Staff Sergeant Anthony Esce also wrote a letter to support Harry Radezky's comments, and added:

I would like to invite special attention to Mr. Radezky's report and especially to the paragraph concerning the departure day of Major Breen. I did not realize it then, but I do now, that we were witnessing the first outward sign that the Major had over reached his physical endurance. Never in all the months we served together had he displayed anything but a cool and cheerful disposition and an ability of meeting all situations correctly and decisively.

In the post-script, Sergeant Esce went on to conclude:

Nervous crack-ups were not too uncommon among officers and enlisted personnel. Captain Stern, Lieutenant Templeton, Captain Plant, Major Sullivan, Corporal Pearson, and many others cracked up and were rotated home for recuperation, many of whom required months of hospitalization. Major Breen took a great deal more of a beating from enemy raids than any of the above mentioned, and he was also overseas for a greater length of time than the above.

Albert Stern also wrote a letter of support in 1952 for my father's medical treatment, commenting that, "Breen's physical stamina held up much longer than did a great many officers and men of our command who were not subjected in any way to the number or type of bombing concentrations—experiences of the advance headquarters unit." Albert also quoted my father as joking after the Bari and Naples bombings and prior to leaving for Rome that he "was feeling nuttier than a ten-pound fruitcake."

While in Rome, my father was finally given orders to return to the States. It had been four very long years, and as no flights were scheduled that day, he was told to travel to the nearest port and take the first available ship home, which turned out to be a hospital ship departing Naples harbor. When the ship finally docked in New Jersey, trains waited to transport the battle weary and injured soldiers directly to the hospital. As my father left the ship and started to walk away, a guard stopped him and asked where he was going. My father replied, "I'm not with these people." The guard was persistent in keeping all patients together on the train, though, and my father ended up at the hospital. The doctors were doubtful of his story that he boarded the ship by happenstance, but promised to investigate. My father lay in bed for two days, wondering how to convince someone to believe him. Finally, on Monday morning, a young doctor called out his name and told him to get dressed—he was free to go.

It took my father a long time to recover from the horrors he had witnessed overseas. When he returned to Dayton, he gave specific instructions that there be absolutely no fuss made over his homecoming. The only person he wanted to meet him at the train station was his mother, Katherine. When his train pulled in, my father's joy and relief were so great that he broke down in tears and cried the entire drive home. In addition, he remained fearful of thunder and lightning for many years, an understandable result of the bombings he endured. Although he never forgot the trials he endured or his comrades in arms who didn't return, my father's emotional state eventually improved and he was able to resume a normal life—albeit older, wiser, and sadder. It was the spring of 1945, and for Eddie Breen, the war was over. Victory was declared in Europe on May 8, and Japan surrendered on August 15. But thanks to the stories he told us and the photographic record he amassed from official army photographers whom he befriended during those trying years, he was able to share the life of a soldier in wartime with those of us who have had to the good fortune to escape such horrific experiences.

MaryLouise

Immediately following the war, MaryLouise remained in Europe where she was appointed head of war relief services in Spain and France for the United States National Catholic Welfare Conference. At the time, there were over twelve million displaced refugees in Europe. An article published on August 30, 1946 described MaryLouise's role and the scope of the post-war problem. [Author note: The publication is unknown.]

NCWC War Relief Services Aids 3 to 4 Millions Victims

Between three and four million war victims have been helped by the War Relief Services of the National Catholic Welfare Conference in France, Miss Mary Louise [sic] Breen of Dayton, director of the program, reveals.

Miss Breen, a daughter of Mrs. John Breen, of Hadley Road, and a sister of Mayor Edward Breen, came home recently on a short leave. February of this year, Miss Breen took charge of the work in France, when the Rev. James H. Toban of the Cincinnati archdiocese had to return to his post on the faculty of Saint Mary's seminary, after a year's absence, during which he directed this war relief program in France.

Miss Breen reports that an average of two million pounds of food and clothing is being received every month in France from the War Relief Services which, she says, bespeaks the great generosity of the American people. One has to see the needy people benefitted by this war relief program to sense their gratitude, Miss Breen is convinced.

What may look like a lack of initiative on the part of the French people in getting back to earning their own livelihood is owing to a number of things which they are unable to surmount, the director says. She pointed to the Vosges department, in the Northeastern section, rich in timber, where mines planted by the armies still make work dangerous.

These mines are holding people back from returning to farming, and France is suffering from a great lack of agriculture. Manpower for farming and other manual work is another handicap. Because of the large percentage of young men physically injured in the war, the farms are being "manned" almost entirely by stooped, old women and German war prisoners.

MaryLouise in her National Catholic Welfare Conference office at the Empire State Building in New York (above) shortly before it was destroyed by a B-25 bomber crash on July 28, 1945.

Charity Nuns Take Charge

"The Sisters of Charity of Saint Vincent dePaul are acting as the distributing agency for the War Relief Services throughout France and they are doing a magnificent job," Miss Breen reports. She says they were chosen for this work because of their familiarity with the country and its needs. Over 800 houses of their community are located in the county.

War Relief Services trucks transport the food and clothing to the distribution centers, where it is distributed under the supervision of the sisters. Miss Breen goes on some of these trips. She says it is hard to imagine the destruction that has taken place in some of these towns.

She cited Caen, which was 65 per cent destroyed, as an example. Only the Sisters of Charity of Saint Vincent dePaul's convent and one other institution in the town remain impartially [sic] intact today, and part of the roof of the former community house was still missing when Miss Breen had occasion to visit it recently.

MaryLouise (center) with orphans and other relief workers, France, 1946.

A report filed in the headquarters at the end of June, showing the number of people and institutions aided by the War Relief Services, includes: 1,554 towns representing 1,962 parishes; 147 hospitals with 39,290 patients; 184 homes for aged, sheltering 25,030; 332 orphanages with a total of 18,399 children; 1,059 holiday camps attended by 114,108 children; 346 infants' homes with 2,545 babies; 106 seminaries; 349 religious communities; 52 prison camps; 49 displaced persons camps.

Besides the food and clothing being sent by NCWC, a number of the local women's councils of the organization throughout American have been sending layettes.

Work Divided into Four Projects

War Relief Services in France is divided into four projects. The first project is caring for the French; the second aids displaced Polish people in France; the third is the Lithuanian project, part of which is distribution of the funds sent over by the Lithuanian committee in the United States. Part of this money is used to send Lithuanians home. The fourth project serves displaced people of all nationalities.

"Headquarters sometimes give you the illusion of Grand Central station, New York," Miss Breen said in referring to

France, January 1946; photo found among MaryLouise's papers after her death. The inscription on the reverse reads, Un souvenir ainsi, ce n'est qu'un au revoir. Merci de votre affectueuse visite et du renconfort qu'ell nous apporte. Terese Vergreete. *Terese Vergreete was one of the nuns with whom MaryLouise worked in France. Her message roughly translates: "A memory [or remembrance] such as this is only farewell [the implication is that the people involved will see each other again and are not saying good-bye forever]. Thank you for your affectionate [loving] visit and for the comfort that it brought us."*

the large number of people of all nationalities flowing in and out of the office. This office has become a crossroads or stopping-off point for chaplains from the United States traveling to and from European countries.

When Miss Breen started home a few weeks ago, the superior of the Sisters of Charity of Saint Vincent dePaul sent the Most Rev. John T. McNicholas, Archbishop of Cincinnati, an authentic relic of Blessed Catherine Laboure, in appreciation of the help which his Archdiocese has given France.

§

Occasionally, MaryLouise returned to New York City for meetings. Her office was at the headquarters of Catholic Relief Services located on the seventy-ninth floor of the Empire State Building. On Saturday morning, July 28, 1945, MaryLouise was at work at her desk; she left the building around 9:00 a.m. to deliver a set of papers elsewhere. Forty-five minutes later she returned to discover that a U.S. Army pilot, Lieutenant Colonel William Smith, had become disoriented from the dense fog and crashed his B-25 bomber into the north side of the building, creating a hole eighteen feet wide and twenty feet high. The Catholic Relief War Office was the main point of impact, and MaryLouise's office was completely destroyed. Eleven of her coworkers were burned to death, some still sitting at their desks; only five, MaryLouise among them, survived. The *New York Times* front page story the following day ran the headline: *Catholic War Relief Office is Chief Victim of Tragedy*, and went on to say that:

An agency that has been in the vanguard of supplying aid and comfort to thousands of homeless and destitute persons in the war zones became yesterday, through one of those curious quirks of fate, the victim of the worst local tragedy of the war.

MaryLouise never fully recovered from the fact that she barely escaped dying that day, and for all the life-threatening situations she had experienced during the war, this one affected her the most. It did not, however, lessen her commitment to her work, and she continued to be affiliated with the agency throughout her life.

§

On April 21, 1953 MaryLouise received Mundelein College's Magnificat Medal to honor her work with war refugees. The award was given annually by this Catholic women's college (now part of Loyola University in Chicago) to a distinguished Catholic college alumna. According to the Saint Mary of the Woods College alumni letter from 1953, MaryLouise "utilized her college training to the fullest, has intensified appreciation for Christian social living by the character of her own life and by her contribution to social, aesthetic, scientific, or religious leadership." MaryLouise was never one to talk about her war time or charity work, but this was an honor she treasured for the rest of her life. Additionally, the French awarded her the Saint Vincent DePaul Medal, which she also highly valued.

My aunt's quiet personality was the opposite of my father's, but her reserved manner did not detract from her concern for human beings in need. MaryLouise's strong Catholic faith influenced her entire life and she spent much of her time working with the Catholic church to accomplish humanitarian goals. She was always willing to help, especially in situations where children were involved, and her acts of kindness, particularly to those in financial need, were frequent and generous, lasting throughout her life. She remained friends with the Catholic nuns that she had met overseas, and she helped them financially recover from the destruction the war had caused in Europe. During the war, she was close friends with the papal nuncio to France, Angelo Giuseppe Roncalli, who became Pope John XXIII in 1958. One of the highlights of her life was taking her husband and niece to visit him at the Vatican in 1959.

Over the Moon

The swearing in ceremony for Dayton's newest and youngest mayor (second from right), January 7, 1946. Eddie Breen was elected mayor of Dayton, Ohio in 1945, making him, at age 37, the youngest man to ever hold that post in the city. The Dayton newspaper headline that day read in part, "City's Youngest Mayor—Single, Handsome, Too." Photo by James N. Keen, copyright Dayton Newspapers, Inc., all rights reserved. Reprinted with permission.

My father had changed while serving overseas and America had changed, too. Once back in Dayton, he hoped to pick up the pieces of his life and resume his work in the hotel business. Having been gone so long, Dad didn't realize that the business as he knew it was done. Many people now owned cars, highways were being built, and a new type of accommodation had emerged—the motel.

Former Ohio governor James Cox urged my father to consider politics, but he resisted. He felt himself to be a hotel man, not a politician. Conrad Hilton, of the Hilton chain of hotels, arranged a meeting with my father in Minneapolis and offered him several positions—California, New York, Florida—but he didn't have any job offers in Dayton. Having been away so many years, my father wanted to stay in his hometown. Mr. Hilton said to him, "When you are in the army, and they tell you to turn right, what do you do?" My father replied, "I would turn right, but I'm not in the army anymore." Mr. Hilton responded, "Well, you're in my army." My father declined and returned to Dayton to look for work. When he didn't find anything, he took Jim Cox up on his offer to run for city commission in the fall of 1945.

Since running for public office was never something Dad intended to do, in many ways he was very naive about campaigning. Luckily, many people he knew from his childhood and the hotel business were eager to help. After talking with Cox, he asked civic leader and community activist Miriam Rosenthal for advice. She wasn't convinced politics was the right direction for him; she also knew that Katherine and MaryLouise, a close personal friend, were adamantly opposed to the idea—all three women were concerned that as a handsome, personable bachelor, he would be subject to scrutiny and besieged in all manner once in the public eye, as he had been to a lesser degree as a hotel manager. But as the prospect of going into politics became more intriguing, Dad also sought advice from his friend Clarence McLin, Sr., a funeral home owner and African American community leader who founded the Democratic Voters League. Years earlier, my father had consulted with McLin about improving hotel employee working conditions, and Dad respected his experience and political savvy. McLin became a positive, supporting influence from the very beginning of my father's political career. [Author note: McLin's granddaughter, Rhine McLin, is the current mayor of Dayton.]

As part of his political efforts, my father went to the "All-Dayton Committee," a group of local business leaders who worked together to help community-minded young men of either party enter the political arena. In those days, the field of competitors was crowded with men returning from the front. And since the candidate who received the most votes for city commission automatically became the city's mayor, the competition was tough and the stakes were high.

§

As it turns out, Miriam Rosenthal's concerns, almost became reality. One evening, after returning to his room at the Biltmore (where he

Former Ohio Governor James Cox and community activist Miriam Rosenthal, above, who along with Clarence McLin, Sr., were largely responsible for launching Eddie Breen's political career. Photo copyright Dayton Newspapers, Inc., all rights reserved. Reprinted with permission.

was now only a guest), Dad received a phone call from an old friend who had moved to Hollywood, married a famous movie actress, and become something of a big shot in the movie industry (unfortunately, his name is lost to time). The couple were planning to fly to Dayton and hoped to meet my father for dinner. Dad thought it was a wonderful idea and agreed to meet his friend's wife at the airport, as his friend was arriving somewhat later. The three decided to meet at a night club just outside the city limits of Dayton. It had a reputation for excellent food as well as illegal gambling.

My father picked up the actress at the airport and took her to the club to wait. They found a quiet booth in the back of the room near the rear door. Dad ordered drinks and they settled in to talk about old times. After an hour had passed, my father and the other patrons heard a loud bullhorn with a man's voice yelling, "This is a raid by the Montgomery County Sheriff's Department. You're all under arrest!"

With that, deputies kicked open the doors, rushed in with their guns drawn, and yelled for everyone to back against the wall. As the sheriff ran in, he happened to see my father out of the corner of his eye. He shouted, "What in the world are you doing in here?" When he saw the actress, he added, "And with her, of all people?" The sheriff instructed the pair to run out the back exit and get in his car, and they did as they were told. As they waited, they saw the local news reporters arrive with their cameras. Soon, the sheriff emerged and drove them back to the Biltmore to wait for the woman's husband. The furious sheriff lectured them the entire drive.

By the next morning, the raid was all over the newspapers. It was a major scandal, not so much because of the gambling, but because so many men had been caught with their mistresses. Several divorces resulted as a consequence. If my father's opponents had known who was also there that night they would have had a field day, and my father's political career could have ended before it had begun.

$

Once my father had committed to running for office, Miriam Rosenthal wrote endless letters endorsing the mayoral candidate. A typical example—and one key to his success—was the following letter addressed to Don Curtner, bell captain at the Hotel Van Cleve:

November 3rd—

My Dear Don:

Eddie Breen is top man on my ticket for city commission. And if you won't consider it an intrusion I would like to shuffle him into first place on your ticket, too.

Maybe it is because his sister Mary Louise [sic] was my close business associate before she went into war service. Maybe it is because I am still stunned by the news that he would be running for city commission. But regardless of why—I have a terrific yen to see him head the ticket Tuesday and your vote for him is something I would like very to have.

Sincerely,

Miriam Rosenthal

Sketch of Clarence "Mack" McLin, Sr. as photographed by Don Black & Associates. He and Eddie became friends in the 1930s when Eddie went to Mack for advice. McLin became an early and strong supporter of Eddie's political career. Courtesy Dayton Mayor Rhine L. McLin.

My father received a huge endorsement on the Friday prior to the election from the over one thousand employees of Dayton's hotels. The Dayton *Herald* reported the story:

The mayoral candidate and his family wish mother Katherine Breen a happy 75th birthday on September 30, 1945 in an event recorded by the Dayton Daily News. *Front row: Mrs. John B. (Catherine) Breen, Becky Breen, Katherine Breen, Johnnie Breen, MaryLouise Breen Garrity. Back row: John B. Breen, Major Eddie Breen, Robert Garrity. Copyright Dayton Newspapers, Inc., all rights reserved. Reprinted with permission.*

Hotel Employes Support Breen In Commission Race

Eddie Breen received an indorsement of his candidacy for city commissioner yesterday that means a tremendous lot to him.

It came from more than 1,000 men and women in the hotel business, employes of the eight Dayton hotels holding membership in the Dayton Hotels association.

They are the Van Cleve, Biltmore, Miami, Gibbons, Holden, Moraine, Beckel and Antler.

Inveigled to come up to the Van Cleve during the afternoon, Breen found a representative group from the several hotels waiting to congratulate him on his nomination and pledge support at the polls next Tuesday.

The city's hotel employees whole-heartedly gave their support to Eddie Breen's political campaign for mayor. Front row, left to right: Frank Kushke, chef, Miami; Ann Martin, waitress, Van Cleve; Major Breen; Berteena Criss waitress, Gibbons; and Joseph Lakatos, chef steward, Biltmore. Back row: Walter Jackson, bellcap, Gibbons; Don Curtner, bellboy, Van Cleve; Bill Hoffman, bartender, Moraine; Jim Cassidy, porter, Biltmore; Hale Roberts, waiter, Van Cleve; Gladys Dabney, maid, Holden; J.A. Jaxson, steward, Biltmore; Robert Primm, room clerk, antler; and Robert Gillam captain of waiters, Miami Flagship. The Dayton Herald, *November 3, 1945.*

Former manager of the Biltmore and Van Cleve hotels, Breen was presented with a bound booklet containing the signatures of the more than 1,000 employes.

"We want to make it known it is our ambition to elect Major Breen to the city commission by such an overwhelming vote he will become mayor of our great city," the employes said in resolutions attached to their names. "We who have had the pleasure of working with Major Breen and under his supervision have found him to be capable, honest, trustworthy, sincere, loyal and cooperative in all of his dealings with us.

"We know that if the electors of this city give him the chance, Major Edward Breen will prove himself a great civic leader, a real friend of the people and a fearless mayor—one of whom all the citizens of Dayton can be proud . . ."

Years later, men such as the Reverend Carlton N. Flanigan remembered how well Eddie Breen had treated them at the Biltmore. In a 1985 *Dayton Daily News* story, Flanigan stated that "there were many who would befriend him [on the road to becoming a pastor], but one in particular stands out—Eddie Breen."

These people also remembered that my father's kindness and fairness was genuine, coming at a time when he wasn't running for anything.

Mayor of Dayton

On election day, November 6, 1945, Eddie Breen received the largest number of votes by a wide margin, thus becoming at age 37 the youngest man ever elected mayor of Dayton. When he was told the good news, he turned to his friend, Al Horstman, and asked, "Where exactly is the mayor's office?" He was not making a joke; his victory was so unexpected that he had never even thought to find out where the mayor worked.

Former Governor Cox wrote to congratulate him on November 13:

I was indeed happy over the election, but I was particularly happy over the decisive majority. I wish your father might have been here to have shared the happiness with your mother and the rest of us.

Indeed, the entire Breen and Beckman clans, for all their worldly successes, were "over the moon" with excitement at Eddie's election.

Mayoral Challenges . . .

Once in office, Mayor Breen decided to begin broadcasting the city commission meetings over the radio so that people at home could listen. Like many good theories, though, it was a disaster in practice. No matter how often my father explained the importance of covering the microphone to say something privately, one elderly city commissioner would constantly forget, leaning over to my father and saying such things as, "Mayor, you'll have to excuse me, I'm going out to take a piss." Every time something like this happened, several angry listeners would call to complain. The plug was finally pulled on broadcasting the

MaryLouise and Katherine congratulate Dayton's newest mayor after his election in 1945. The photo on the table is of his father, John P. Breen, holding son Henry who was killed in an accident in 1899. Photo copyright Dayton Newspapers, Inc., all rights reserved. Reprinted with permission.

meetings after the city commission debated a filter system for a new public swimming pool. The same commissioner pronounced, "Hell, Mayor, I don't know why we need to waste money on a filter system. When I was a boy we'd jump into the old Erie Canal and pop out of the water with horse turds on our heads. It never bothered anyone and we're all alive and healthy today!" When listeners heard that, the radio station switchboard lit up like fireworks on the Fourth of July.

As Dayton's mayor in the post-war era, there was no need to ask what the city needed, because the answer was "everything." Everything had been rationed and nothing replaced during the war years, so when he requested items such as new fire trucks or police cars, they were funded without argument. Men returning from the war needed jobs, so he could also hire people and expand city services without controversy. The only real problem he encountered was when he decided to move the Civil War statue of Private Fair that stood at the end of Main Street. Moving the statue across the river to Sunrise Park wasn't actually the problem—most people recognized it would create traffic problems in

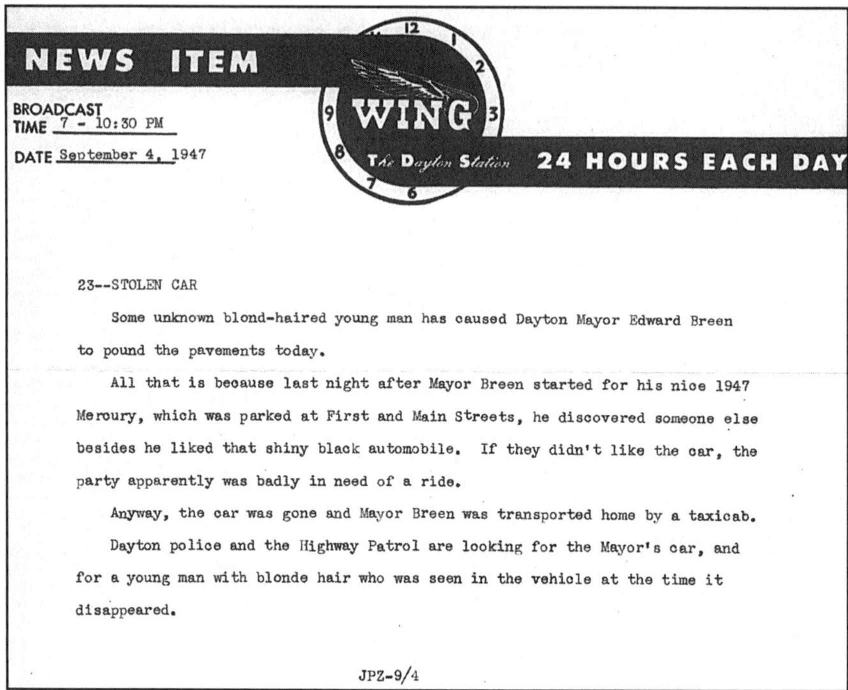

NEWS ITEM

BROADCAST TIME _7 - 10:30 PM_

DATE _September 4, 1947_

WING

The Dayton Station — 24 HOURS EACH DAY

23--STOLEN CAR

    Some unknown blond-haired young man has caused Dayton Mayor Edward Breen to pound the pavements today.

    All that is because last night after Mayor Breen started for his nice 1947 Mercury, which was parked at First and Main Streets, he discovered someone else besides he liked that shiny black automobile. If they didn't like the car, the party apparently was badly in need of a ride.

    Anyway, the car was gone and Mayor Breen was transported home by a taxicab.

    Dayton police and the Highway Patrol are looking for the Mayor's car, and for a young man with blonde hair who was seen in the vehicle at the time it disappeared.

JPZ-9/4

When a mayor's car is stolen, it's news. Story
by Jack P. Zeigin for WING, September 4, 1947.

the future if left in its current location. Instead, problems arose when a newspaper reporter asked my father which way the statue would face in its new location. The new mayor acknowledged that he had never thought about it. When his comments were published the next day, the arguments began. It seemed as though everyone in town had an opinion—some said it should be facing toward the city; some said it should stand with its back to the South. A few suggested it face west and watch the sun set, while others said it should face east and watch the sun rise. The newspapers took advantage of the growing controversy and published as many opposing comments as they could. The radio stations played it up, and on some nights my father would be awakened at one or two in the morning by some drunk at a bar calling to offer his view.

Finally, as my father was walking down the street one morning, former Governor Cox walked up to him, tipped his hat and this exchange ensued:

"Good morning, Mayor. Which way are you going to face that statue?"

One of the benefits of being mayor was an invitation to ride in the Indianapolis 500 pace car with two lovely models, obviously not the gentlemen shown here. Courtesy IMS Photo.

"Darned if I know."

"Have you ever seen a statue that doesn't face the sidewalk?"

And with that, Governor Cox walked off and thus the decision was made—the statue would face the sidewalk.

. . .And Mayoral Benefits

MaryLouise was living in New York at this time and had begun dating Robert Garrity, whom she met at an officers' club dance. In her letters home to her mother, MaryLouise would write, "Mr. Garrity picked me up at the train station and dropped me off at my hotel here in New York" or, "Mr. Garrity drove me to the theater last night." Back in Dayton, Katherine told all the ladies in her garden club that MaryLouise had finally hired a chauffeur. A few months later, Katherine received a letter saying, "Mr. Garrity has asked me to marry him and I have said yes." Katherine was so upset that she called my father: "The chauffeur has

The Mayor walks his sister, MaryLouise,
down the aisle, February 18, 1947.

just proposed marriage! As mayor, can you contact the FBI and have this Mr. Garrity investigated? It is very inappropriate for a chauffeur to ask his employer to marry him!" The next day, my father informed her that Mr. Garrity had always been MaryLouise's boyfriend, not her chauffeur. Escorting her down the aisle while mayor was a personal highlight of his tenure in office.

Boy Scouts, Part II

Soon after becoming mayor, my father commented to a dinner companion that he had once been a Boy Scout, but had quit back in the early 1920s while he lacked only the cooking badge to become an Eagle Scout. He vowed to rectify the situation. So on July 19, 1946, with reporters and troop leaders following him, my father donned a scout uniform and went out to the local Boy Scout camp, where he built a fire

Milton Caniff cartoon above showing Dayton Mayor Eddie Breen completing his Eagle Scout Badge. From A History of the Boy Scouts of America in the Miami Valley Council, *courtesy Miami Valley Council Boy Scouts of America. Below, Mayor Breen cooks for local scoutmasters. Copyright Dayton Newspapers, Inc., all rights reserved. Reprinted with permission.*

Orville Wright's homestead, Hawthorn Hill, is located in Oakwood, Ohio, close to Dayton. The home is now owned by the National Park Service. Photo thought to have been taken by Orville or his sister, Katherine Wright. Courtesy Dayton Public Library.

and cooked a meal. For his efforts, he was awarded the Eagle badge and the scouts received a great deal of publicity. Dad had a deep love and appreciation for the Boy Scout organization all of his life, and some of his fondest memories came from the many scout camping trips he had taken. He was still going on scouting trips with my brother and me into his late sixties and early seventies, and always claimed that many of the skills that he learned while scouting helped him through the difficult war years.

Orville Wright

My father had known Orville Wright since his childhood at the Phillips Hotel when Wright often dined there, giving Dad candy. As mayor, he occasionally went to the aviator's home, Hawthorn Hill, for dinner. Those dinners were rather solemn affairs as Wright was a quiet, subdued man. Carrie Kayler, Orville's devoted, longtime housekeeper, was always very pleasant and my father could rely on having a lively conversation with her, even if Wright himself didn't say much. It didn't hurt that Carrie was an excellent cook and well known for the pies that she baked.

Orville Wright circling over Dayton in one of his early biplanes, September 22, 1910. Steele High School is in the background; the Civil War statue of Private Fair that Mayor Breen had moved to the opposite side of the Miami River is the tall white obelisk at the far end of the bridge (it was moved back just prior to his death in 1991). Courtesy Dayton Public Library.

Orville Wright was known as a man who rarely gave speeches. One night over dinner my father asked him why, and he replied, "Eagles can fly, but can't talk; parrots can't really fly but can talk; so I just think I'm an eagle."

Wright's pet project was to have the proposed air force academy built in Dayton, but he met with a great deal of opposition. Reportedly, the generals at Wright-Patterson Field were not keen on having a swarm of college kids nearby, and many congressmen from Western states complained that the other service academies were all in the East. In March of 1949, shortly after Orville Wright died, my father managed to get a bill before the House of Representatives calling for an air force academy in Dayton. The bill had the support of the entire Ohio delegation, but went down in defeat. Instead, Colorado Springs, Colorado, was chosen.

When Orville Wright died on January 30, 1948 at the age of seventy-seven, my father, as mayor, was one of many who became an honorary pallbearer. The honor of carrying Wright's casket was something he always remembered. He never understood the number of businessmen

Army Day Parade, April 9, 1947. Mayor Breen is next to the woman on the left; Orville Wright is the second man on the mayor's left. Photo copyright Dayton Newspapers, Inc., all rights reserved. Reprinted with permission.

who called his office to complain about the funeral procession passing down Main Street. They were worried it would disrupt their businesses, and wanted the route changed. My father refused, arguing that Orville Wright deserved to be carried through the heart of the city he loved.

UNITED STATES CONGRESSMAN

After three years as mayor, Dad decided to run for United States Congress. Laurence Newman, an associate editor and columnist for the *Dayton Daily News*, later wrote about this period of my father's life in a 1987 column:

> *It's worth remembering that his sense of principle was such that when he declared his candidacy for Congress, he resigned as mayor "in view of the fact that Dayton's municipal government is non-partisan. . . so that neither I, personally, or the office represented can be embarrassed at any time by the impropriety of partisan indulgence." The words may have sounded lofty, but they told us a lot about the man's character.*

When Orville Wright died in 1948, Mayor Breen served as an honorary pallbearer; he is in front on the right with one hand on the casket and one hand holding his hat. Courtesy of Special Collections and Archives, Wright State University.

The Campaign

By today's standards, my father's campaign was unusual. Television advertising was virtually unheard of, and speeches broadcast on the radio or transcribed in the newspaper were the most common means of mass communication. Dad became the first local politician to do a television interview, but because many people living in rural areas in 1948 did not yet have electricity much less television, his audience was mainly limited to those living in town.

Luckily, he had the strong support of former Governor James Cox, because he also faced a primary battle within the Democratic party. It was a mark of the esteem in which she held him that in February of 1948, Miriam Rosenthal, the much admired community activist who served as secretary-treasurer of the Breen-for-Congress campaign office, wrote of her concerns to former Governor Cox:

> *. . . there is a mistaken notion that Eddie has unlimited resources of his own to sink into the election. This not true. We must remember that on top of a war service record, Eddie has given better than two years to the city job which he has done at no small financial sacrifice. He has much at stake in trying to put his insurance business on sound footing. If he isn't objective about it he is liable to fall into the old pattern of the public servant who ends up with his hand out for a lift. It isn't fair to maneuver Eddie into this position.*
>
> *All of this of course is a very personal matter and I am taking the liberty of elaborating on it with you knowing what your sensibilities would be—and knowing that at the proper time you will bear down upon the proprieties to the proper persons in this campaign. If we are in earnest about electing Eddie, something should be done soon to put an anonymous discretionary fund at his disposal so he can be relieved of bread-and-butter worries and put all of his thinking on ways and means of piling up votes for the Washington deal . . .*
>
> *Seriously—as we have discussed before—it is rare that politics has an Eddie Breen. If we are interested in doing a job we shouldn't take anything for granted. He's going all out. The rest of us who claim to be interested, should do no less.*

[Letter courtesy of the Special Collection and Archives, Wright State University and held at the Paul Lawrence Dunbar Library at Wright State which houses the James Cox papers.]

The "Give 'em Hell Special"

An unusual campaign opportunity arose when my father was invited to ride on the "Give 'em Hell Special," President Harry S. Truman's campaign train. Truman's aides knew that my father had been in the hotel business and was acquainted with a great many people, so he was asked to join them when the train arrived in Cincinnati on October 11, 1948. My father was to provide the president with names of people in small Midwestern towns so that Truman could fit the names into his speech and make it more personal. In exchange, Truman would add a plug for my father's campaign.

CITY OF DAYTON, OHIO

EDWARD BREEN
MAYOR

January 14, 1948

Honorable James M. Cox, Publisher
The News
Miami, Florida

Dear Governor Cox;

Tomorrow I plan to enter the competition for United
States Congressman from this district.

So that my indulgence in partisan politics will in no
way embarrass our non-partisan municipal government,
I have asked the Commission to act favorably upon my
request for retirement from the Commission and from
office of Mayor by April 15, 1948. This allows ample
time for the selection of a permanent City Manager.

Needless to say I have wished more than once since the
subject of running for Congress has come my way that I
could walk down to Fourth and Ludlow Street for the
most expert counsel there is. I look forward to imposing
upon your good nature in this regard the next time we
meet. Maybe you won't object to a short shop talk at
that time.

I wish you a very pleasant season in Florida and most
cordial greetings to both you and Mrs. Cox.

                        Sincerely,

                        Mayor
EB:gcw

*Letter informing Governor Cox of Eddie Breen's
resignation as Mayor to run for congress.*

The News League
Dayton, Ohio

THE DAILY NEWS		THE DAILY NEWS
DAYTON, OHIO		SPRINGFIELD, OHIO
THE DAILY NEWS	THE JOURNAL	THE DAILY SUN
MIAMI, FLORIDA	ATLANTA, GEORGIA	SPRINGFIELD, OHIO

Miami, Florida

OFFICE OF THE PUBLISHER

January
20th
1 9 4 8

My dear Eddie:

This replies to your letter of the 14th.

You will have every ounce of strength I can give
you not only because you deserve it, but there
will be a push added now and then in memory of
your father for whom I had great affection.

Now make up your mind to follow your conscience and
do not set your sails exclusively or semi-exclusively
to the winds of expediency. Think things out and do
what ought to be done for the good of your country.
You will find this will promote self respect always.

Sincerely,

James M. Cox

Honorable Edward Breen
Mayor
Dayton, Ohio

*Governor Cox's letter of support for Eddie
Breen's candidacy for the U. S. congress.*

My father agreed, and went to Cincinnati. He stayed overnight at the
Netherland Plaza to be sure he would not miss the train and early the
next morning he was directed by campaign aides to a small room where
he could wait for the president. He sat down beside an older man reading the newspaper and after a sip of coffee Dad turned to the man and
said, "They tell me the old man is going to be on the train today." With
that, Truman put down the paper, which had obscured his face, and

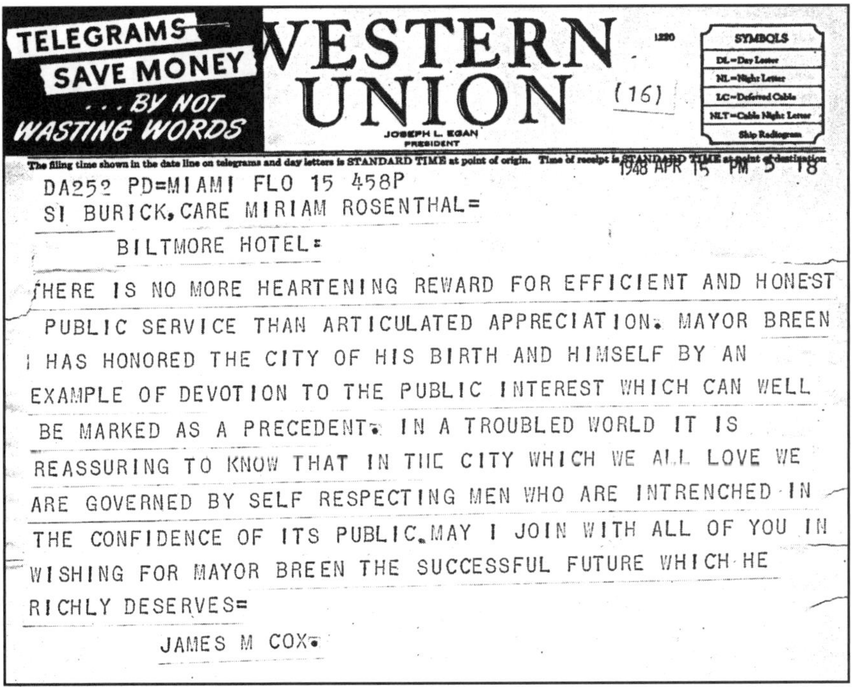

*Telegram from former governor James M. Cox to Miriam Rosenthal
in support of the Breen congressional campaign, April 15, 1948.*

said, "Yes, I think I will." My father was very embarrassed, but he found
Truman to be a warm, friendly man right from the start. Through politics and travel, Truman knew many hotel owners in cities around the
country, so Truman and my father shared bond.

When the train left that morning, my father found himself sitting
with Mrs. Truman and her daughter, Margaret, while President Truman
and his aides sat across the hallway. Their first stop was Hamilton, Ohio,
and Truman walked to the back platform of the train with my father
standing behind him. Truman began his standard speech about voting
out the 80th Congress—"This is a do-nothing Congress, and you need
to elect good young men to the next Congress, such as my good friend,
Eddie Green,"—then slapped my father on the back. At each stop, the
president continued to refer to my father as "Eddie Green," but my
father was too embarrassed to correct him. Finally, in Middletown,
Ohio, a newspaper man who knew my father followed him back into
the train. "If the president calls you Eddie Green in Dayton," said the

President Truman's October 30, 1948 motorcade through downtown Dayton. Congressional candidate and former mayor Eddie Breen is in the front seat between two Secret Service agents. President Truman is shown in the back seat (left), with former Governor James Cox beside him. Photo copyright Dayton Newspapers, Inc., all rights reserved. Reprinted with permission.

reporter, "you two will be a laughingstock." My father realized this was true, and told one of Truman's aides of the mix-up. By the time they got to Dayton, the correction was made.

Still, Dad had one more misconception to clear up. Since he had been sitting with Mrs. Truman and Margaret on the train, rumors flew that this handsome bachelor was dating the president's daughter. He persuaded some of the national reporters on the train to tell the local reporters that there was no basis to the story. My father knew that Truman was a very strong family man and he didn't want a false rumor to ruin his new friendship with the president.

Once the train arrived in Dayton, a parade was scheduled and my father was to sit in the backseat of the open car with President Truman and former Governor Cox. Late the night before, a phone call jarred him awake and the voice on the other end of the line said, "If you ride

President Harry S. Truman, City Commissioner Fred Speice, candidate for Ohio Governor Frank J. Lausche, former Governor James M. Cox, City Commissioner Roy Neth, and United States Congressional candidate Edward G. Breen after traveling with Truman on the "Give 'em Hell Special", October 11, 1948. Copyright Dayton Newspapers, Inc., all rights reserved. Reprinted with permission.

down Main Street with the president, I'll blow your head off." My father called the Secret Service and reported the threat; they told him to move to the front seat so they could better protect him. The next day the car made its way uneventfully down Main Street. When it stopped to allow Truman to give a short speech, however, a friend of Dad's noticed him turn around and engage in what looked like a very deep discussion with Cox. Years later, the friend asked my father what the two of them had been talking about, thinking it had something to do with the death threat. My father laughed and said Cox had tapped him on the back and said, "Did I ever tell you that I knew you worked at Harding's home when I was running against him?" Cox was anything but upset—in fact, he found it amusing. He just wanted my father to know that the secret the Breens had been keeping for years wasn't really a secret at all.

Whether his experience with Truman's Give 'Em Hell Special was beneficial is open to debate, but my father won his race for the Third Congressional District by a wide margin and was elected a member of the Eighty-first Congress. Several days later, he received a letter from former governor Cox, with words that he took to heart:

> *. . . now make up your mind to follow your conscience and do not set your sails exclusively or semi-exclusively to the winds of expediency. Think things out and do what ought to be done for the good of your country. You will find this will promote self-respect always.*

Issues and Colleagues

The issues facing Congress in the late 1940s and early 1950s included the Korean War, early civil rights legislation, Joe McCarthy and the spectre of communism, as wells as statehood for Alaska and Hawaii. The Eighty-first Congress included notable members such as Helen Gahagan Douglas (Democrat, California); Gerald R. Ford (Republican, Michigan); John F. Kennedy (Democrat, Massachusetts); Richard M. Nixon (Republican, California); Franklin Roosevelt, Jr. (Democrat, New York); and Adam Clayton Powell (Democrat, New York), who was first elected to the Seventy-ninth Congress and was one of only two African-Americans serving.

New members of the Senate included Wayne L. Morse, at the time a Republican from Oregon (he became an Independent in 1952 and a Democrat in 1955), later famous for giving the then-longest filibuster in senate history; and Hubert Humphrey, former mayor of Minneapolis and a close friend of my father's from their days as mayors of sister cities. My father admired Humphrey, later vice president under Lyndon Johnson. Their friendship proved fortuitous. They were frequent lunch partners during Dad's tenure in Congress and often informal liaisons between the House and Senate.

Dad also got along very well with Adam Clayton Powell, whom he assisted with early civil rights legislation. Washington, D.C. was still a segregated city in 1948. My father could never understand how a government that preached "liberty and justice for all" could be discriminatory to people on its own doorstep. He also saw it as a slap in the face to the many black veterans of World War II, including the Tuskegee Airmen he so admired. Adam Clayton Powell, although he was a United

Congress of the United States
House of Representatives
Washington, D. C.

November 1, 1950

Mr. Morris H. Simmons, President
NAACP
1020 West Fifth Street
Dayton, Ohio

Dear Mr. Simmons:

As you undoubtedly know, I am one of the two members of the
Negro race elected to the present 81st Congress.

I would like to say a few words in behalf of the present
Congressman from your District, the Honorable Edward Breen,
(Democrat) of Dayton, Ohio.

I have watched Mr. Breen's work during the two years he has
been in Washington and can state that he has proved under
fire to be a true friend of the American Negro.

I believe you will readily recall that Mr. Breen took part in
that memorable 16-hour session in the House of Representatives
last February during which time my bill was debated.

Mr. Breen, along with myself, was among that small group of
178 Congressmen (from a total of 435 members in the House of
Representatives) which voted against an amendment which "pulled
the teeth" from the Fair Employment Practices bill. This vote,
which occurred at 3:17 a.m., clearly demonstrates Congressman
Breen's sincerity on FEPC.

I believe it would be to the best interest to the members of
the Negro race in the Third Ohio District to keep such a man
as Mr. Breen in Congress. He is a Congressman who has proved
under fire to be a friend of the American Negro.

Sincerely yours,

(signed) Adam Clayton Powell, Jr., M.C.
Twenty Second District, New York

Letter from Congressman Adam Clayton Powell, Jr. to the president of the Dayton chapter of the NAACP in support of Eddie Breen.

States congressman, could not enter many of the restaurants on Capitol Hill, nor was he was permitted to use the barbershop designated for House members, although he ultimately integrated many of these facilities. Many restrooms and hotels were off-limits to him as well. Powell could not ride in taxis, and if he chose to take the bus, he had to sit in the rear. According to House doorkeeper William "Fishbait" Miller in his autobiography *Fishbait*, Representative Powell was not allowed to swim in the congressional pool, and when he did jump in, Fishbait received several complaints.

My father believed in challenging those rules. When black constituents visited him in Washington, he would often invite the visitor to lunch in the congressional dining room, as he would any other constituent. Many times, he would walk black constituents to the street corner and personally arrange for a cab to spare them embarrassment. When college students from nearby Howard University (often the children of constituents) visited his office, he made certain they had a chance to walk out on the House floor and sit in the speaker's chair. He wanted them to feel that the speaker's chair represented all families in America, not just white families.

In a personal letter written in November 1950 to a Dayton community leader who was the local chapter president of the NAACP, Congressman Powell strongly endorsed my father's re-election bid.

Personal prejudices and opinions often influenced congressional sessions. One congressman from the deep South, John Rankin of Mississippi, strongly disliked Representative Powell simply because he was black, and the dislike was mutual. My father recalled that Powell made it his mission in Congress to sit next to Rankin every day. If Rankin moved his seat, Powell moved also. This went on for quite some time. One day, as they were debating a school desegregation bill, the animosity between them exploded into a maelstrom of racial slurs. My father recalled the tirade going something like this:

Representative Rankin, going on for ten or fifteen minutes: "If this bill passes my wife will be forced to go to P. T. A. meetings with 'niggras,' my children will have to go to school with 'niggras' and I don't want any white children to have to go to school with 'niggras.'"

Representative Powell: "Mr. Speaker and distinguished members of the House, I deeply resent the remarks of the previous speaker. He should be censored for calling my race 'niggers.' I resent him calling my wife and children 'niggers.' No man should have to sit here and be insulted like that."

Representative Rankin (looking directly at Representative Powell): "Mr. Powell, I never called you a 'nigger.' I never once referred to your race as 'niggers.' You, sir, are a liar and you can even go so far as to have the house clerk read back my statements and you will see that I am not

Congressman Breen in 1950 with his long-time secretary, Grayce Ward (far left), and visiting constituents Mary June Simpson (near left) and Mary Ann Wilken (far right). Photo courtesy of A. P. Images.

wrong. What I did say, Sir, was 'niggra': your wife is a 'niggress' and your race is 'niggras.'"

Fists started flying, and my father said books and papers scattered in every direction. The Sergeant at Arms had to be called to restore order. (A similar incident is recounted in *The Political Biography of an American Dilemma* by Charles V. Hamilton.)

Fist fights were, unfortunately, rather common when debates became heated. Dad once saw one elderly Jewish gentleman jump over a table and punch another representative in the face when debating the formation of Israel. Sometimes even the page boys ended up participating.

§

One of the most reliable people on my father's staff was his generous and capable head secretary, Grayce Ward. Grayce worked with him from the beginning of his political career in Dayton and remained with him until the end of his congressional career. It was Grayce who came to Washington soon after the election and set up my father's office in the hallway; because the office they were assigned to was still in use by the previous congressman. When they eventually moved into official quarters, Grayce ran a tight ship, keeping the office running in an efficient, yet relaxed manner.

As a bachelor, my father received a great deal of attention from single women. Much of it was unwanted and one of Grayce's responsibilities was to act as a buffer. Many of these women would send my father framed pictures of themselves or large flower displays. Dad always tried to be diplomatic and gracious, but it was Grayce's job to see that the pictures were returned and the flower displays sent to a local hospital. Many years later, Grayce recalled that some women didn't take the rejections well. Often, they became extremely nasty. Others tried to trick Grayce into revealing my father's home address, or his favorite restaurant. A few even phoned Katherine in Dayton, which truly annoyed my father. Grayce, though, was always very protective and would never reveal anything. She remained close to my father until the end of his life and to the family thereafter.

§

Of all the famous, infamous, and interesting people my father met during his years in Washington, he most enjoyed William "Fishbait" Miller, the House doorkeeper. Fishbait was a farm boy from Pascagoula, Mississippi, who came to Washington at a young age to work for a Mississippi congressman and ended up staying forty-two years— twenty-eight of them as the doorkeeper. Some people didn't take him seriously since he was a bit short and chubby, wore his hair slicked back with grease and spoke with a thick Mississippi accent. But my father enjoyed his friendship and all the stories he had to tell. As Dad

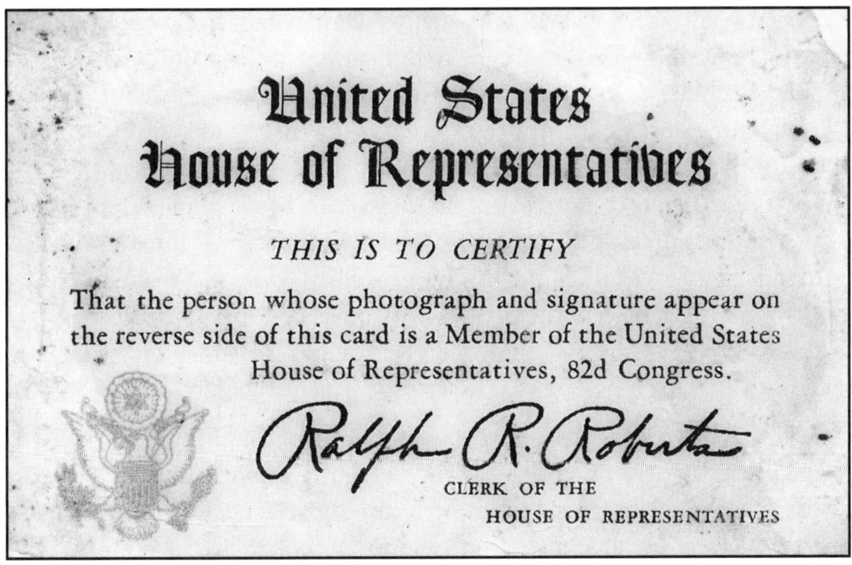

Eddie Breen's congressional identification card.

recalled years later, Fishbait had a heart of gold, and he was always more than willing to help people find solutions to their daily dilemmas.

Fishbait always said that if he left his position on his own terms he would never write a tell-all book, but if he left on someone else's terms, he would write a book revealing everything. Politics being politics, he left Congress in the mid-1970s, but not on his own terms after a wave of new Democrats failed to retain him, preferring a less anachronistic image. Fishbait wrote his autobiography, and told all he knew; after twenty-eight years, he knew a great deal.

§

In 1950, Dad ran for re-election against Republican Paul F. Schneck and won by a landslide. It was the first time in over twenty years that a candidate from his district was re-elected; supposedly, the seat held an anti-reelection curse. When Dad won, Dayton newspaper headlines read, "Breen Beats Bugaboo; Returns in Off Year!" The article noted that, "What's more he's a liberal Democrat with a perfect Fair Deal voting record." (The district was heavily Republican.) The article went on to say that, "He conducted a clean, hard-hitting campaign. Ed Breen is a credit to the people who believe in him, and to the people he represents in Congress." As with the many other situations and opportunities in my father's life, this clearly showed that he was truly "Lucky Eddie".

Dad usually met weekly with fellow Democrats to have lunch and discuss upcoming legislation. He greatly enjoyed these luncheons, as he missed his close friends from Dayton. Representative John F. Kennedy and Senator Hubert Humphrey were part of this group, and my father liked both men very much. He became good friends with Jack Kennedy, not altogether surprising as they were both single, Democrats, and Irish Catholics with similar wit and personalities. Kennedy was first introduced to my father by a neighbor and old friend from his hotel days, George Mead, Sr., the president of the Dayton-based Mead Paper Company whose son had once been Kennedy's classmate at the Choate Academy.

During these luncheons, some of the men, including my father, would arrive early because they knew that Kennedy and Humphrey would always be late. As wealthy as Kennedy was, he seldom picked up the tab for the meal, so it became a game to concoct an elaborate plan to get him to pay. No matter how clever the plan, Kennedy always managed to get away without paying the bill, although nobody really cared because they all liked him so much. With Hubert Humphrey, the goal was to try and trap him into an argument, as Humphrey prided himself on being able to talk his way out of any situation. As hard as they tried, Humphrey, too, always outfoxed them.

Once, my father was dining with Jack Kennedy and another congressman who was also a veteran of World War II. Dad mentioned that he had received another death threat, and admitted to his lunch companions that these were starting to disturb him. Kennedy replied that they had all lived through the war, and if they were going to get killed, it would have happened then. My father recalled that Kennedy firmly believed they had survived because they had a destiny to fulfill. He advised my father not to worry—what would happen, would happen.

Dad thought about that conversation many times after Kennedy was assassinated in 1963. He was very sorry to see him die in such a violent way, but he also said that he understood how Kennedy felt about life and death, and knowing that gave him a sense of peace. Jack Kennedy was one of the men my father most admired, and he was grateful for the short time he knew him.

The Inaugural Committee

requests the honor of the presence of

Honorable Edward G. Breen

to attend and participate in the Inauguration of

Harry S. Truman

as President of the United States of America

and

Alben W. Barkley

as Vice President of the United States of America
on Thursday the twentieth of January
one thousand nine hundred and forty-nine
in the City of Washington

Please reply to
The Inaugural Committee
Tariff Building
Washington 25, D. C.

Melvin D. Hildreth
Chairman

Invitation to the 1949 inauguration of President Harry S. Truman

THE TRUMAN FAMILY

Another person whom my father enjoyed knowing was J. Vivian Truman, the president's younger brother. A farmer in Missouri, Vivian came to Washington several times a year. The White House staff never really knew what to do with him—often they would tell him to go to

Capitol Hill and report back any interesting news. My father knew it was a ruse, but he never minded Vivian's visits. He thought Vivian was a good man, and he had many interesting, humorous stories to tell. Vivian was very proud of his brother and very devoted to him, even though the two lived vastly different lives. A reporter asked their mother, "Are you proud to have a son sitting in the White House?" She replied, "Yes, I am, and I am just as proud of my other son who lives in the farmhouse down the road."

However, there was one person of whom my father was not overly fond—Mrs. Madge Gates Wallace, President Truman's mother-in-law. Although they only met a few times, those few times were enough. My father had an appointment at the White House at the time when President Truman was deciding whether or not to fire General MacArthur. As Dad was walking into the president's office, Mrs. Wallace was stepping out. She said, "Congressman, Harry thinks he has the right to fire General MacArthur." After she left Truman made a joke of it, but to a man steeped in manners, this lack of respect was abhorrent. Truman was very good about letting his mother-in-law's barbed comments slide by, but even he found a few incidents difficult to ignore, such as when Mrs. Wallace told the press that she knew Harry Truman all too well and that's why her vote would be for Thomas Dewey, Truman's opponent. Even Truman's critics gave him high marks for tolerating this woman.

During the early 1950s, there was a serious housing shortage in Washington, and in the nation as a whole. Because of this, my father shared an apartment with a man who happened to be a boyhood friend of Truman's. Once a week, if the president was in town, my father's roommate would play cards at the White House with the president and several of their old friends.

The burning question in 1951 was whether Truman planned to run for re-election in 1952. Over breakfast one morning, the roommate, who had played cards at the White House the night before, announced that, "Harry's not going to run next year." Truman hadn't said anything about the next election, but had admitted that his near assassination earlier that year had affected his wife, Bess, more than the American public knew. The man went on to say he had known Harry all his life and that if something affected Bess Truman that much, Harry Truman wouldn't run. His intuition proved to be correct.

§

THE WHITE HOUSE
        WASHINGTON

                                        April 16, 1952

    Dear Ed:

            It was fine of you to write to me as you
    did concerning my announcement at the Jefferson-
    Jackson day dinner that I shall not be a candidate
    for re-election. I appreciate to the full your
    high evaluation of the leadership I have given my
    country and your personal words of gratitude.

            Mrs. Truman and Margaret share my cordial
    thanks for your good wishes for the years ahead.

                    Very sincerely yours,

                    Harry Truman

    Honorable Edward Breen,
    101 Hadley Road,
    Dayton,
    Ohio.

President Harry S. Truman's letter thanking Eddie Breen for his support.

On the day that General Douglas MacArthur's separation from the military became official, my father was called to Speaker Sam Rayburn's office an hour before MacArthur was to appear before Congress. He and several other men were assigned to talk to MacArthur before he gave his speech. The meeting was kept rather informal. Dad had invited his niece, Becky, and nephew, Johnnie, to come to Washington to hear MacArthur. A few days before the meeting, however, the Republicans voted to prohibit family members from the House floor. Because of his friendship with Fishbait, Dad was at least able to usher the two children into his office, where he and they listened to the speech on the radio. He felt it was more important to keep his promise to his niece and nephew than to be on the House floor for what was essentially a ceremonial event, albeit an historical one.

RETIREMENT FROM CONGRESS

A man with the last name of Brehm was a congressman at the same time as my father. Both men were from Ohio, but from different political parties. Naturally, the similarity of their names caused a tremendous amount of confusion. Telephone operators constantly misrouted calls and my father was often blamed for Republican votes cast by Mr. Brehm. Mr. Brehm, in turn, was held responsible for the Democratic votes cast by my father. The men's offices were far apart from one another, and tourists with a short amount of time in Washington would become upset if they were steered in the wrong direction.

The breaking point came when radio commentator Drew Pearson added to the confusion. The following newspaper clipping described the story:

> Slip On Name By Pearson Causes Stir—It wasn't Dayton's Edward Breen. A mispronounced name set Daytonians buzzing Sunday night as Drew Pearson dropped a 'bombshell' in his 6 p.m. broadcast from Washington. In his 'predictions of things to come,' he said something which sounded like this: 'A supporter of Sen. Taft, Ohio Congressman 'Breen' will be investigated for salary kickbacks.' Many Dayton listeners were as amazed by the first part of the statement as the last part. Dick Cull of The News Washington Bureau was sure he knew the explanation but called Pearson for confirmation. Pearson was referring to Rep. Walter E. 'Doc' Brehm of Millersport in the 11th Congressional district - not Rep. Edward Breen of Dayton. He had pronounced the name as 'Breem,' instead of correctly as 'Brame,' a common mistake in Washington, Cull explained. Pearson, whose column appears daily in The News, will write a column on the Brehm charges this week. Late last night Miriam Rosenthal, secretary-treasurer of the Breen-for-Congress campaign office, announced she would ask Pearson to correct last night's misinterpreted broadcast during next Sunday's radio commentary. Miss Rosenthal said her phone rang constantly with Dayton radio listeners who had mistaken Brehm for Breen.

Cox always referred to his neighbor Eddie Breen's house as an "ugly covered bridge." Breen home photo by Robert Thompson.

The mix-up was a horrible experience for my father and, as he admitted later, one of the reasons he decided to retire from national politics. In the 1950s, most Americans still received their news from listening to radio commentators such as Pearson, whose show was heard across the nation, and they tended to believe what they were told without question. On the day the story broke, my father was flying to Dayton from Washington and he didn't know what had happened until landing, when reporters asked him for a statement. Once inside the airport, he was hounded by angry Dayton citizens as well: "I always trusted you to do the right thing and it turns out that you are just as crooked as everyone else." "My husband and I always pointed you out to our son as someone to emulate, and now you've disappointed us. We don't know how we can tell our son what a louse you turned out to be." Another man got so worked up he tried to spit on my father. It was a nightmare.

He went straight to Miriam Rosenthal, and they called in two lawyers who sent a blistering letter to Drew Pearson, threatening to sue and demanding an immediate apology. My father and Drew Pearson had always gotten along well, so in addition to the political fallout, he was hurt that Pearson would have given such a scathing news report without checking the facts more carefully. The following Sunday, Pearson devoted his entire Sunday broadcast to my father and explained the mix-up to his listeners. In fact, he went out of his way to explain how valuable Ed Breen's work had been to the United States Congress.

The whole controversy turned out well, but it deeply bothered my father that people could turn on him so quickly and so viciously. As for Drew Pearson, the two remained good friends for the rest of their lives. My father was never one to hold a grudge when someone made a mistake but made it right, as Pearson had done.

In 1951, my father made the decision not to seek a third term in congress, and to resign near the end of his second term. He had been feeling ill for quite some time, with symptoms of dizziness and double vision. His doctors concluded he was suffering from nerve damage caused by his many wartime concussions. That explanation sounded plausible, and for the next fifteen years it was the basis for his treatment. Then one day in 1969, while spending the summer in Maine, he collapsed to the ground, unconscious. He was rushed to the hospital, where he was diagnosed as a severe diabetic. The doctors in Maine were astounded he had never been tested for the disease because he exhibited all the classic symptoms.

My father's retirement from politics disappointed many people, but most understood his reasons. Speaker of the House Sam Rayburn wrote this on July 3, 1951:

Dear Ed: Thanks for your note of June 27th. I deeply regret that the condition of your health necessitates your retirement from Congress. If you had been in good health, I am sure your splendid ability and fine character would have taken you far and brought about a brilliant record. It will be a great pleasure to see you any time you come this way.

With every good wish for you always, I am Sincerely yours, Sam Rayburn.

P.S. I received your other letter stating you were going to resign effective October 1, 1951. Of course you will have to make this resignation to the Governor of the State and at that time I will lay down your letter.

James Cox's home, Trailsend, *pictured above, was built in 1916 and intentionally resembles the White House, which Cox had hoped to occupy one day. Photo copyright Dayton Newspapers, Inc., all rights reserved. Reprinted with permission.*

HOME

Back in Dayton, my father's doctors told him to take long walks for his health. One day, as he was walking on a high ridge near the home of Governor Cox, he met an old high school friend. They stopped to talk and the friend mentioned that he was dividing the land they were standing on to be sold for future home sites. With subsequent encouragement from Governor Cox, my father bought a tract, and designed and built the first and only home he would ever own in the Dayton area. Built to fit into the hillside, the house from the front appeared to be two-stories but from the back it looked more like a one-story ranch. Even with his poor health, my father's sense of humor remained. The developer had named the street Echo Spring Trail—after his favorite bourbon—and that became the only bourbon my father served at his dinner parties.

As my father was overseeing the finishing touches on his house, he looked up one day to see Governor Cox watching from his property line. My father invited him over for a closer look, but Cox said, "No, thank you. I can see it all from right here. It looks like a G-- D-- ugly covered bridge!"

Katherine Breen died in her home in Oakwood in 1953 at the age of eighty-three. Her sons Eddie and John were with her when she passed away. Although my father and his mother were close and spent much time together, my father was rarely lonely after her death and his retirement from national politics. He had business interests to look after and many friends, plus his old army buddy, Albert Stern, lived in the lower level of the house for months at a time. Years later, Albert told me, "The saddest day of my life was when your father married your mother and I had to go back home to my wife." Charles Kettering, the founder of Delco and inventor of things as diverse as the all-electric starting ignition for automobiles, Freon, and anti-knock gas, lived about a block away, and he and James Cox would sometimes walk up my father's driveway, throwing small pieces of gravel against the windows to get his attention. The three of them would sit on the patio overlooking the city and talk politics or about Dayton in days gone by.

Back then, Dayton was a community of neighbors helping neighbors. People believed that the better a person or neighborhood was, the better it made the nation as a whole. National pride was an important aspect of everyone's character in the post-war 1950s, and people did all they could to make Dayton a better place.

Most Eligible Bachelor No More

Eddie Breen and Connie Focke married on November 10, 1956. Photo copyright Dayton Newspapers, Inc., all rights reserved. Reprinted with permission.

One Friday afternoon in early August, 1956, my father went to the barber shop for his weekly hair cut. As usual, he arrived at 1:30 and sat next to his good friend, Irvin Harlamert, Sr. On this particular day, the two happened to be discussing the rising cost of meats, and their discussion turned to the Focke family, owners of a local meat company. Irvin suggested my father meet Elmer Focke's daughters, whom, he reported, all had good personalities—plus, they could cook and sew. Irvin gave him the Focke's phone number and mentioned that my father might have seen the oldest daughter, Connie, since she sold dresses downtown. My father recalled a rather attractive young woman working in the dress department back when his mother was alive, and decided to call and ask her to dinner.

My father had been involved with the Focke family two years earlier, after he left Congress. Mr. Focke—Elmer—had called him to ask for the names of several people in Washington whom his wife, Marie, could contact. Connie had been in a very serious airplane accident and was in a hospital in Arlington, Virginia. According to the *Dayton Journal-Herald*:

> An Oakwood woman was injured seriously yesterday (May 7) when struck by a propeller of a private plane at Marshall, Virginia. Miss Constance Focke, 26, had just alighted from the plane. She was on her way to the Gold Cup Steeplechase at Warrington, Virginia, with a group of friends. She was reported in unsatisfactory condition at Arlington, Virginia hospital last night. Miss Focke is the daughter of Mr. and Mrs. Elmer J. Focke of 1150 Oakwood Avenue. Her father is treasurer of the Focke Packing Company of Dayton. Her mother flew to Arlington yesterday after hearing of the accident. She reported today her daughter is "in as good condition as can be expected." Mrs. Focke said her daughter was hit on the head, above the eye and on the back. Her right arm was badly lacerated and the bone shattered. "The doctors now say they believe they can save the arm,'" Mrs. Focke said. "They say that it has a pulse. The doctors say they believe she is on her way to recovery'" . . .

Despite my father's previous help in the matter of Connie's accident, my maternal grandparents were not overly fond of him upon their first meeting. All they knew was what they had read in the newspaper, but there were two things that stood strongly against him—he was Irish and a Democrat, while they were staunch German Republicans.

My parents dated only once before they decided to marry, reminiscent of John P. and Katherine's similar quick decision a half century earlier. When my mother told my grandfather after this first date that she was engaged, he phoned my father that very night. He, along with the entire Dayton community, had always believed my father would be a lifelong bachelor. However, my father assured him that he had heard quite correctly. The whole family was caught off guard by the quick marriage proposal—after all, my father was forty-eight years old and my mother was twenty years younger.

In a way, it seemed my parents had been destined for each other. The Focke family's housekeeper claimed to be a palm reader and fortune

CITY OF DAYTON, OHIO
OFFICE OF THE CITY COMMISSION

MUNICIPAL BUILDING • THIRD AND LUDLOW STREETS • HE-3441

COMMISSIONERS
HENRY S. STOUT, Mayor
HOWARD R. MALONE
R. WILLIAM PATTERSON
EDWARD V. STOECKLEIN
ROBERT L. SCHELL
CLERK OF COMMISSION
OSCAR F. MAUCH

PROCLAMATION

WHEREAS, in the span of time as all things come to pass, Edward Breen, bachelor, and Constance Focke, spinster, have decided to file a joint income tax return; and

WHEREAS, Miss Focke has accepted Mr. Breen's proposal to become a deductible item; and

WHEREAS, the Bureau of Internal Revenue will suffer a body blow at 12:30 p.m., Saturday, November 10, 1956.

NOW, THEREFORE, I, Henry S. Stout, Mayor of the City of Dayton, Ohio, do proclaim Saturday, November 10, 1956 to be CONSTANCE and EDWARD DAY and do order as follows for a proper observance of the occasion:

1. All citizens shall fly Confederate flags from their TV aerials.

2. At 1:00 p.m., all ex-flames of Congressman Breen, suitably attired in sack cloth and ashes, shall gather at Third and Main and proceed in solemn procession to Calvary Cemetery.

3. That the bristles in all street sweepers shall be removed and replaced with pink ostrich feathers - the sweepers are to follow the mourners and clean up the ashes.

4. All street flushers to be emptied and replaced with Chanel No. 5 or "My Sin".

5. All fire engines to be repainted passionate pink to suitably reflect Mr. Breen's mood.

6. Box 21 and other rescue squads are to be stationed at all bridges to restrain all Miss Focke's suitors who tried and failed.

IN WITNESS WHEREOF, I have hereunto set my hand and the Seal of the City of Dayton this 9th day of November, 1956.

Henry S. Stout
MAYOR OF THE CITY OF DAYTON, OHIO.

*A tounge-in-cheek proclamation in support
of Eddie and Connie Breen's marriage.*

teller. When my mother was about five years old, the housekeeper told her that someday she would marry a boy who lived three blocks away. Although mother and my grandmother gave this much thought, they could not think of any boys that lived in the vicinity. At that time, though, my father did live three blocks away. Because he was so much older, his name never occurred to them.

*Eddie Breen and Albert Stern in 1956 on the evening
before Eddie and Connie's wedding. Eddie and Albert
met as soldiers in North Africa during WWII and their
friendship lasted throughout the rest of their lives.*

November, 1956 was a busy month for my father. Not only did he and
my mother marry, but he was also elected to the Montgomery County
Commission where he was to serve twice as president. It was the last
time he served in public office.

Connie Focke's horse, Lady Mac, was shod while held by her riding instructor, King Tullis, circa 1939. On her wedding day, Connie carried the buttons from Tullis's vest in a blue velvet bag. Copyright Dayton Newspapers, Inc., all rights reserved. Reprinted with permission.

MARRIAGE AND HONEYMOON

My parents' wedding ceremony took place on the tenth at Holy Angels Catholic Church in Dayton. On her wedding day, for something blue, my mother carried hand-painted buttons in a blue velvet bag. The buttons were a gift from her former riding instructor, King Tullis, who had remembered her saying to him when she was seven years old that she wanted the buttons from his vest when she married. She had always admired them and was delighted and surprised when he handed them to her just before she walked down the aisle, some twenty-three years later.

In the months leading up to the wedding, my parents arranged to travel to Tegucigalpa, Honduras, and then to Mexico City for their honeymoon. They were both looking forward to a romantic and exotic time, but as the wedding approached, Honduras broke out in revolution. The U.S. State Department issued a warning that the area would not be safe for travelers. My father, never one to back down from a challenge, decided to keep their plans. The day after the wedding, my parents flew to New York City and caught the S. S. *Ancon* to Panama, then continued by plane to Honduras. (My maternal grandmother believed they were only going to Mexico, because no one wanted her to worry.) When the plane landed in Tegucigalpa, my parents were the only two to leave the cabin. Years later, my mother recalled the other passengers staring curiously, perhaps thinking they were missionaries, as who else would voluntarily visit a country in the middle of a revolution? On their way to the hotel, they passed soldiers marching with machine guns, and when they reached the hotel, the front desk clerk told them they shouldn't have come. In addition, he informed my parents that the hotel staff did not feel safe staying at the hotel overnight . . .did my father know how to use a gun? When my father answered affirmatively, the man handed him a pistol and advised him to move the dresser in their room against the door.

That night, barricaded inside their hotel room, my parents heard frequent gunfire and shouting. My mother was frightened but my father, who had seen much worse during the war, wasn't greatly bothered. As they sat and looked out the window of their room, Dad explained to my mother that the flashes they were seeing were tracer bullets. Usually, he told her, every third round was a tracer bullet so that the shooter could see where the bullets were going. In addition to the sound of the bullets, there were also many explosions. My mother declined her new husband's lesson in pistol handling "in case anything happens to me if someone breaks in." But this was their honeymoon, after all, and the violence and turmoil did little to lessen the excitement about their future life together.

The next morning, the sun shone and all was quiet. The hotel staff returned and served them a large breakfast, and later, a guide took them on a tour. They drove around the beleaguered city and in the afternoon, the guide gave them a tour of the city jail. My mother said the jail was full to capacity, quite dirty, and smelled very bad. Although this was not exactly what she had imagined for a honeymoon, she later admitted it was very exciting, and certainly made her appreciate the things she had always taken for granted.

After two days in Honduras, the Breens decided they'd had enough of revolution. Mexico City was a nice change and they finally had a good night's sleep. Touring the city, they saw posters advertising a bull

*Eddie Breen surrounded by children while
on his honeymoon in South America.*

fight, and thought that it might be fun. Returning to the hotel that evening, Dad inquired about tickets. The concierge informed him they were impossible to obtain, as it was the year's biggest and most highly advertised bull fight; in fact, the fight had been sold out months ago. My father thanked him, but just as he was about to walk away he turned and casually asked where the best travel agency was located. After learning it was only a few blocks from the hotel, Dad thanked the man again and he and my mother returned to their room.

Early the next morning, my parents went to the travel agency. Dad asked to see the manager, and solemnly said, "My name is Edward Breen and I am here to pick up my tickets to the bull fight." My mother was shocked, but remained silent. The manager replied, "I'm sorry, but we don't have any tickets here for you." My father angrily replied, "What do you mean? They have to be here." The man proceeded to look all over the agency and ask the other employees, but of course no one could locate the tickets. Finally, he asked my father, "Who told you that we would have the tickets here?"

"The American ambassador to Mexico."

The manager became very flustered, apologized profusely, and asked for an hour to find out what happened. My parents left, and halfway down the block my mother said, "I can't believe you would do something like that!" My father just laughed.

An hour later, they returned to the travel agency. This time, my father walked in alone. My mother waited outside, afraid they would be arrested, hauled off to a Mexican prison, and never heard from again. When my father went to the front counter the manager was waiting and with a smile of relief handed Dad a white envelope embossed with the seal of the American Embassy. The manager repeatedly apologized for the mix-up. My father coolly answered that mistakes happen, and he'd recommend this travel agency to his friends back home.

The next day my father and mother were escorted to front row seats by an official from the Mexican government. There, they discovered that they were sitting in the seats reserved for the American ambassador and his family. Afraid to press their luck, they didn't inquire as to his whereabouts. My mother was amazed by the whole episode. She was just beginning to discover that life with my father was going to be very interesting.

I was born the following year, and my brother, Robert, followed eleven months later. With a young family, my father decided to slow down and enjoy time with his wife and children. His own childhood was nothing more than a distant memory, and it was time to pass along all he had learned and experienced to a new generation. When I was ten, my parents adopted a five-year-old girl, Cynthia, completing our family.

Summers in Maine

In 1959 we began vacationing each summer in Maine, close to MaryLouise and her husband, Bob Garrity, who had settled there permanently after the war. My father had been under a great deal of pressure to run for senate, governor, or perhaps even vice president, on at least two separate occasions. The first time was around 1950 after his strong second term re-election to Congress when both former Governor Cox and House Speaker Sam Rayburn wanted him to try for higher office. Because it coincided with his declining health, resignation from Congress, and return home to Dayton, however, it was out of the question.

The second time was in 1960, three years after Governor Cox's death, and this time the source was a large group of businessmen in

Bass Harbor Head Light, Bass Harbor, Maine near the Breen summer home on Mount Desert Island. Photo by Robert Breen.

Cleveland and Youngstown, Ohio who were beguiled not only by Eddie Breen's past political successes but also by his new storybook family.

By this time, my father had no interest whatsoever in a national political career with its time demands and Drew Pearson-like incidents. Nonetheless, the pressure became so intense that my parents went so far as to consider living in a diplomatic community in Mexico. Meanwhile, the Garritys wanted them to move to Maine. My father still felt needed in Dayton, particularly with the early civil rights movement beginning, and so he settled on taking our family to Maine from the end of May until the first week of September. He would stay a week, fly home for three weeks, fly back to Maine for two weeks, and return to Dayton, finally making one last visit in September in order to drive home with us. The pattern was enough to convince Ohio's political power brokers that he meant what he said: he intended to spend time with his family, his community and his business interests, *not* building a national political career, flattering though the opportunity might appear to be.

After my father fully retired in 1969, he abandoned the commuting routine and began spending the entire summer in Maine.

In 1962, my parents built a home on a large lake on the coast of Maine, and this became my father's true love in the latter part of his life. The property bordered Acadia National Park, meaning there were vast amounts of undeveloped forest to the left of the home, and to the right, only an abandoned log cabin no one had used in years. With so much privacy, it became Dad's habit to wake at 5:00 a.m., don a thick terry cloth robe, brew some hot coffee, and go for a lake swim. Even in midsummer the water in Maine is cold, so he typically brought his coffee with him. And since the rest of the family was still asleep, he rarely bothered with a swim suit. One foggy morning, after following his usual routine, he was sitting on a large flat rock sipping his coffee, waiting to dry before putting on his robe. Suddenly, a woman in a rowboat appeared out of the fog. Rowing nearer, and without acknowledging his appearance, she announced that she was "your new neighbor" and that she and her husband had just bought the log cabin next door. My father was shocked, but carried on a polite conversation and now, forty years later, our families are still friends who joke about the incident. The rock from which he used to skinny dip has become a legend of sorts to our family and visiting guests. Many of our guests have continued with the tradition of swimming *au naturel* and once, a local newspaper society columnist dutifully reported one such scandalous episode.

*The strong spirit that MaryLouise exhibited in her younger days
(she's shown here after earning one of her many equestrian trophies at
Dayton horse show in the 1930s) lasted well into her later years.*

In 1987, Laurence Newman, a former associate editor and columnist for the *Dayton Daily News*, and a close friend of my father, wrote a column about those summers:

> For years it was his custom to ask friends by the dozens to join him in a Memorial Day cookout. With an energy that seemed boundless, he'd oversee the grille and the bar and dash from one cluster to another, making sure no one lacked anything. Then, when he felt he could relax for a minute, he'd talk, when urged, about his concerns in local government or in politics or his days as a hotel manager or as associate of Miriam Rosenthal or, if really pressed, as a square dancer who, ever so briefly, could allemande left with the best. This was also a time to talk about the summer vacation his family would be taking in Maine, in a house he had designed on a wooded lakeshore lot on Mount Desert Island. To Ed and his wife Connie, it was especially enjoyable to compare vacation plans with friends who had visited them in Maine and who shared their love of the outdoors. Ed would list the mountains they would climb,

the places they would see by boat, or by land, and most important, the activities he would become involved in with his sons, Eddie and Bob, and his adopted daughter, Cindy. Married at 48, after having been one of Dayton's most eligible bachelors for years, Ed made it his mission in life, as he reared his youngsters, to concede nothing to age in his 50s, 60s and 70s. It was his duty, he felt, to teach his kids about self-reliance and personal achievement, by example as well as by word. To a visitor 25 years his junior, Ed's nervous energy often seemed intimidating even though he didn't mean it to be. There was no mountain climb, no all-day hike that Ed couldn't manage. There was no day, from June to September, when Ed would find it too cold to plunge into the water, just a few feet from his Maine home. There was no time he would be too busy to initiate a bewildering variety of activities for adults and youngsters alike, from morning to night. Age, to Ed, was but a state of mind, and he fiercely refused to make the first concession.

§

MaryLouise had the same attitude toward life. When she was in her mid-eighties, my brother and I took her out on the lake for a sailboat ride as my father watched from the shore. A strong gust of wind flipped the boat, throwing us all in the water about a half mile from the nearest shoreline. In a matter of minutes, my brother and I had righted the small boat and climbed back in, but MaryLouise simply could not pull herself on board, even with our help. Finally, she told us she would swim back, which she did. It was a distance that most eighty-year-olds could never have managed, especially in the frigid Maine water. And as my father pointed out when she reached the dock, not once did the straw hat that she had been wearing come off her head! Although this experience would have deterred most people from ever sailing again, MaryLouise was out on the boat with us the very next day.

Even now, years later, I have remained friends with many of the Dayton families that summered near us in Maine. In those days, we would all picnic in a secluded spot near the ocean and eat boiled lobsters and native Maine corn from the garden of the local game warden, Don Cote. For those who didn't care for lobster (I was one of them), there would be steak, chicken, or hot dogs. Blueberries were always hand picked early in the morning and made into pies and muffins for the evening picnic. After eating, we children would run along the

*Long Pond, Mount Desert Island, Maine, where the
Breens built a summer home. Photo by Robert Breen.*

shoreline gathering shells, starfish, and whatever else was to be found along the rocky beach. After dark, there was always a contest to tell the best ghost story.

Daily life on the island was carefree. The older generation regularly attended quieter affairs such as luncheons, cocktail parties and bridge clubs, while the younger generation enjoyed water skiing, sailing, canoeing, and mountain hiking. But by mid-afternoon or early evening, our various groups would come together.

My uncle, Bob Garrity, belonged to the Pot and Kettle Club, which dated back to 1899. Its sixty-five to seventy members included former U.S. vice presidents, diplomatic officials, international heads of banking, railroad presidents, and various CEOs of industry. It was members-only, and there were no signs advertising where it was located along the shores of Frenchman's Bay. Famous guests entertained at the Pot and Kettle Club included Harry Truman, John Kennedy, and Admiral Richard E. Byrd. Bob was also on the Northeast Harbor Town Council and a member of the volunteer fire department, so while none of us would ever be considered "locals", we always felt more a part of the community than many of the summer residents did.

§

Another notable local spot favored by the area's social set was the Jordan Pond House where MaryLouise and Bob often went for tea and popovers following Sunday mass. The original farm house was built in 1870 and still in use during the Garritys time. Tables were set up on the lawn, a strict dress code existed in their day, and it was as elegant as you would expect. One of the more curious aspects was the special table set apart for the chauffeurs so that they, too, might enjoy a glass of lemonade and, if really lucky, a popover, although not amongst their employers. John D. Rockefeller, Jr. bought the property in the 1940s to protect it from development (it adjoined his estate), and a small group of local people have operated it since 1946. Unfortunately, the original building was destroyed by fire in 1979. I vividly remember helping to work the fire line that night. The Jordan Pond House still exists, now open to the public and still serving their famous popovers, but not nearly so formal as in MaryLouise's day.

My aunt's permanent home was just a few miles outside of the town of Northeast Harbor on property her husband had purchased after the war. It was a magnificent custom-built house that sat high on a granite ledge overlooking Somes Sound. Guests were enthralled by the stunning views of the sound and the hand-crafted furniture by George Nakashima—the wood from her dining room table even had a silver bullet still lodged inside of it. Her friend Helen Thompson, wife of Pittsburgh steel magnate David Thompson and owner of a famous summer home, Saheda, nearby, had several Nakashima pieces that inspired MaryLouise and Bob to contact the furniture maker. In turn, MaryLouise told me that Nelson Rockefeller admired her furniture at a luncheon she and Bob gave, so much so that he ordered over two hundred pieces to be handcrafted by Nakashima for his home in Tarrytown, New York.

MaryLouise spent summer days tending her large garden and entertaining friends and relatives. She often took them to visit the nearby Abby Aldrich Rockefeller Garden, which in midsummer was spectacularly colorful. Another favorite spot was the elegant and intimate Asticou Gardens, famous for its Japanese sand garden and hundreds of azaleas. Both the Abby Aldrich Rockefeller Garden and the Asticou Gardens have Asian themes, but the Rockefeller Garden is much larger, with many huge stone statues. It is surrounded by an eight-foot tall reddish Chinese wall, with some of its tiles taken from a section of the Peking wall. Beatrix Farrand, a noted landscape architect who lived on

The Jordan Pond House lawn as it appears today. Photo by Robert Breen.

the island in the 1920s, designed the gardens with the help and advice of Mrs. Rockefeller.

To my aunt's pleasure, some of the visitors who especially enjoyed the gardens were three of the French nuns she had met during World War II. These brave women had helped her to find the radios hidden in the French countryside that she used to communicate with Allied forces.

Just off the shoreline of MaryLouise's Northeast Harbor home lay a small island. Both my father and my aunt loved to swim there, and encouraged my brother and me to do the same. We were usually reluctant, as the ocean was freezing even in midsummer, but there were rare occasions when we joined them.

In high school, my friends Bob Williams, Quintin Smith and I sometimes rowed out to the island and spent the night. Once, we saw hundreds of falling stars—so many that my friend Bob, who had lived in the city all his life, was convinced we were witnessing a UFO invasion rather than a meteor shower. As an hour passed, we began to think that perhaps he was right. The next morning we woke up, tired and still unsure of what we had seen, when my uncle and aunt came down to the shoreline, made a large breakfast for us, and we all ate next to the ocean.

At age ninety-one, MaryLouise left Maine and returned to Ohio, where she died in a nursing home on September 2000 at the age of 96, far from the ocean she loved. While there, she enthralled the staff with her stories, including tales of visiting the ancient Egyptian tomb of King Tutankhamen soon after it was discovered and opened. To me, it seemed out of character for her to reveal her past, but perhaps in her old age she found comfort in revisiting memories, even to strangers. Certainly, she had outlived many of her contemporaries with whom she had shared her adventures. The nursing staff remembered her fondly— a very proper, dignified matron who continued to dress for dinner right until the end.

One particular incident at this time also gave me a glimpse into the war years that she rarely discussed. When *Saving Private Ryan* was released in 1998, I offered to take her to see it. She declined in no uncertain terms, explaining that she had been in the editing room at the American Embassy in Madrid when the raw film taken during the first three days of the D-Day invasion was screened. Even though over fifty years had passed, she told me that the faces of those dead young men hanging upside down from the cliffs on the beaches were still vivid in her mind. While she was not in the editing room for this reason and wouldn't divulge what the reason was, she did say that secretly, she was looking for, and hoping she wouldn't find, the face of her brother.

MaryLouise died in the same way she lived her life, with tenacity and strength. Her remains were scattered near her husband's, who had died five years earlier, on a mountaintop in Maine overlooking the ocean.

§

Bar Harbor, Northeast Harbor, and nearby Seal Harbor, at the turn of the twentieth century and well before that, were home to many of America's luminaries, including Joseph Pulitzer, John D. Rockefeller Jr., George Vanderbilt, the Carnegies, the Astors and, later on, Edsel Ford, the son of Henry Ford, and Edward Stotesbury, senior partner at J.P. Morgan & Co. They all built beautiful summer homes on the island, and Bar Harbor acquired a reputation as the place to summer for the high society set. Unfortunately, a large fire in 1947 destroyed many of Mount Desert Island's grand homes and only a few remain today.

Although it didn't happen often, there were occasionally reminders that life in Maine wasn't always so sophisticated. One such incident occurred the night I attended a formal cotillion in Northeast Harbor. On

Game warden Don Cote and wife Bea entertaining in the late 1960s at one of the annual "Hoot and Holler" parties the family threw for friends and family to celebrate another summer together. Each family put on a skit in addition to the Cotes' playing and singing.

the way home I hit and killed a deer. Dressed in ball gown and tuxedo, my date and I walked to a nearby farmhouse and called MaryLouise. She arrived at the scene in bathrobe and curlers, at the same time as the game warden. My date and I had already decided to keep the deer—I would keep the head and legs, she would use the skin for a rug, and we would share the meat. After finishing the paperwork, the game warden put the deer in my trunk and left; we followed MaryLouise to her home. My aunt fetched flashlights and a knife and my date, still in her formal gown, offered to gut the deer. (I was relieved because I didn't know a thing about gutting a deer.) Once finished, we loaded the deer into my car and drove it to my house, placing the carcass on a shelf outside my parents' bedroom window. Her dress and my tux were by then inde-scribable.

The next morning, my parents woke to an awful smell. When my father climbed out of bed, he looked out the window and saw the deer head staring straight back at him. He was shocked, to say the least, although a few days later, he had recovered sufficiently for us to hold a large party to eat the venison.

§

Friend and game warden Don Cote's rugged good looks (he was voted best looking game warden in Maine several years running) became familiar to millions of Americans in 1968, when he appeared in a commercial for Camel cigarettes. In the commercial he walked down a foggy Maine beach, sat in a chair and propped up his feet, showing a hole in the bottom of one of his boots. Then, in his thick Maine accent, he exclaimed, "I'd walk a mile for a Camel." This became the brand's marketing slogan for years.

Don took care of the residents of Mount Desert Island where we lived. Barbara Behrendt described Don's life in a *Bar Harbor Times* pro-file on August 8, 1963:

> The title of fish and game warden is a bit misleading, because the job entails many more things than merely safeguarding the island's fish and game. Cote leads a kind of jack-of-all trades life, being a policeman, a detective, a dog catcher, a forest ranger, a boat inspector, a house inspector, a water policeman, and a public speaker, all rolled into one. And, like a doctor, he is on twenty four hour call, seven days a week.

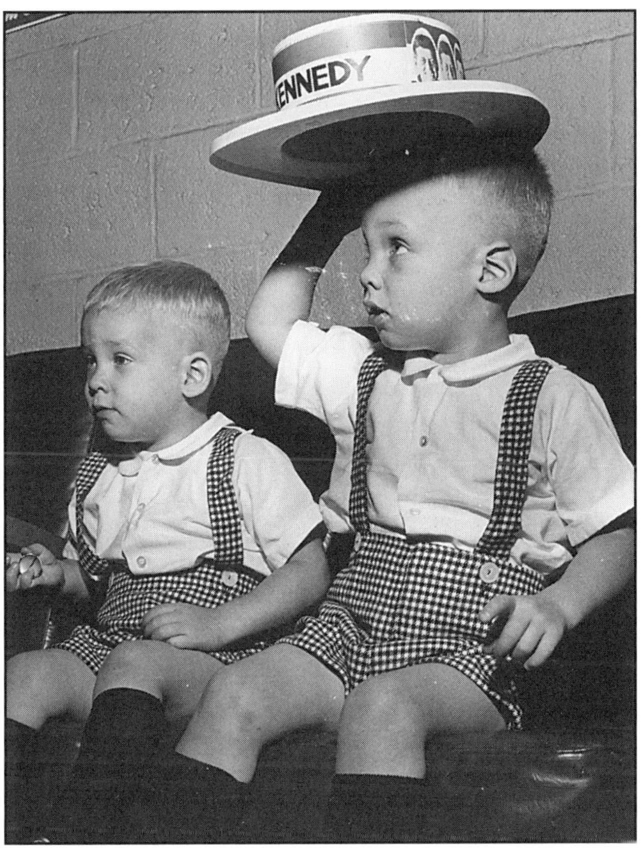

The author (right) and his brother, Robert, stumping for John F. Kennedy during Kennedy's stay at the Dayton Biltmore Hotel, October 17, 1960. Photo taken in the lobby while their father was meeting with Kennedy upstairs. Copyright Dayton Newspapers, Inc., all rights reserved. Reprinted with permission.

§

Each year when we arrived back home in Kettering in early September it would be time for my brother, sister, and I to start another school year. My father returned to his work as an advisor with the Montgomery County Commission, and my mother would resume her many volunteer projects. But we all kept another year's worth of memories from our summer in Maine.

DAYTON VIGNETTES: *The Candidate Kennedy Comes to Town*

On October 16, 1960, Senator John F. Kennedy, then the Democratic candidate for president, flew into the Dayton airport on a small private plane. Along with other dignitaries, my father, who was in his last year on the county commission, was on hand to greet him. After a short impromptu speech from the senator, the group got into several cars and followed Kennedy to the Manchester Hotel in Middletown, Ohio, where Dad was able to say a few words to his former colleague. Returning to Dayton the next day, Senator Kennedy gave a speech at the Biltmore Hotel; it was the last time my father saw his friend in person.

Years later, Robert Daley, a reporter for the *Dayton Journal-Herald* who covered the visit, told me:

> *I was a young reporter at the time covering my first presidential campaign. I was impressed that Ed Breen, a man whom I knew and who had a leading role in the political life of our community, was on a first-name basis with a presidential candidate. Although I saw President Roosevelt ride by in a caravan in Youngstown, Ohio during World War II and had covered a speech by President Eisenhower in Cincinnati, I had not known anyone who actually knew a presidential candidate. I was a few feet away when John Kennedy and Ed Breen shook hands and chatted. That day was memorable to me.*

Two Mayors

One spring morning in April 1960 Dad drove to Chicago for a meeting. City and county officials from around the country attended to discuss the different ways large cities could dispose of toxic waste. On his way to the meeting, as he drove through the small town of Knightstown, Indiana, a police officer pulled him over for speeding. Because he was driving many miles over the speed limit, Dad had to go to downtown Knightstown and appear in person at traffic court. Once there, the judge peppered him with questions, including where my father was employed. Dad replied that he was the mayor of Dayton, Ohio—neglecting to add that he had been mayor fifteen years earlier. The judge ruled to let my father off without a fine, but gave him a warning to watch his speed in the future. Dad assured him he would, thanked the judge, and left.

Ironically enough, two hours later, the current mayor of Dayton, R. William Patterson, drove through Knightstown. He, too, was pulled over for speeding and appeared in court in front of the same judge. Asked for his occupation, he replied that he was the mayor of Dayton. The judge took off his glasses in disgust, looked right at him and said, "Tell me sir,

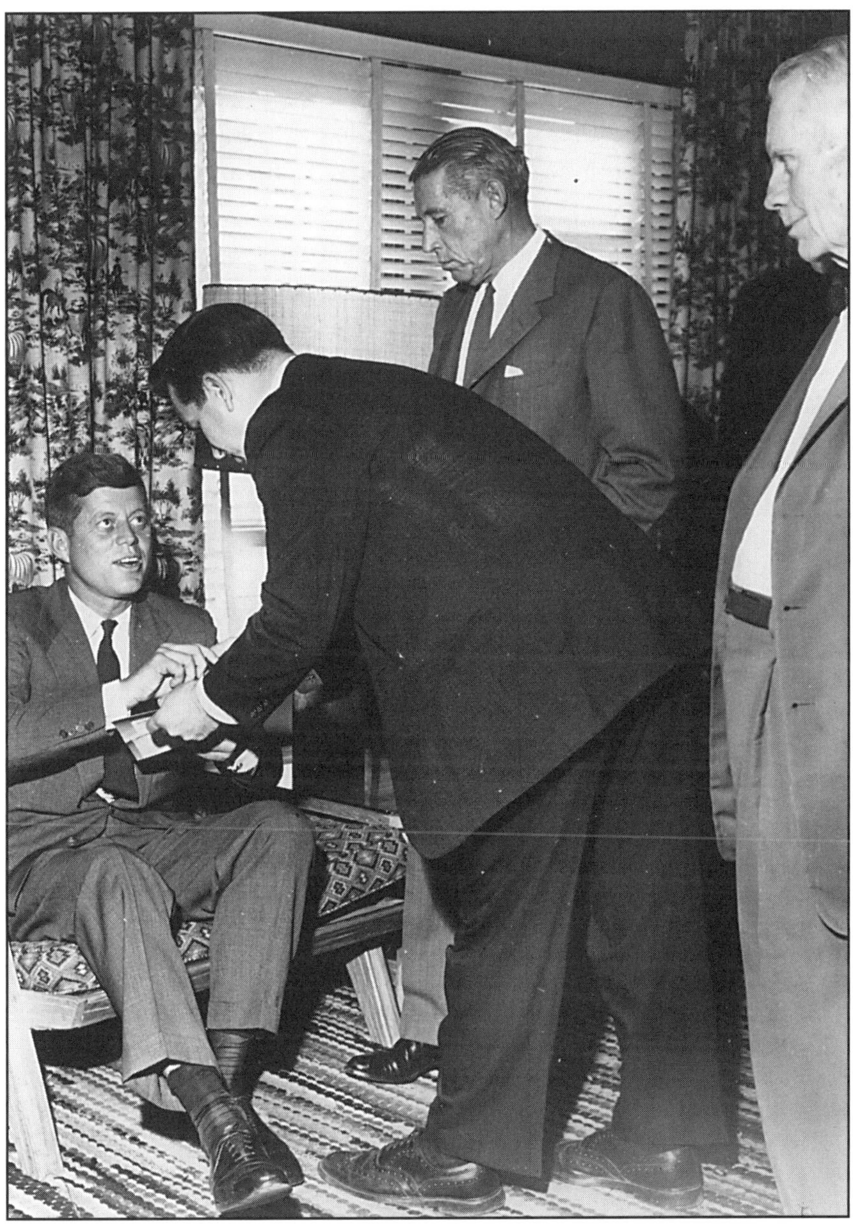

John Kennedy campaigning for president in Dayton on October 17, 1960; it was the last time that Eddie Breen had an opportunity to renew his acquaintance with the future president. State Representative Robert Roderer is shown getting an autograph. Looking on are James M. Cox, Jr. (center), son of the former governor, and Albert Horstman (right, partially visible), Montgomery County Democratic Chairman. Copyright Dayton Newspapers, Inc., all rights reserved. Reprinted with permission.

how many mayors does your town have?" Patterson replied, "Just one, and I'm it." After a long pause, the judge explained that there had been a man earlier in the day who claimed to be Dayton's mayor. Since my father was gone and there was nothing the judge could do about him, he decided instead to fine Patterson the maximum amount.

Several years later, my father happened to be seated next to Patterson at a dinner party. During the course of the meal, Patterson turned to my father and said, "Hey Eddie, have you ever driven through Knightstown, Indiana?" When my father answered, "Why, yes, and I got a speeding ticket," Patterson told him what had happened. For years, it was a big joke between the men.

The Sheriff

During this same time period, one of our neighbors, Wayne ("Moose") Morse started calling my father "the sheriff of the neighborhood," because he would walk the family dog down the street after dark. Dad was even given a real sheriff's badge. From there, given my father's love of entertaining, it evolved into a party—every time a family went on vacation, my parents threw a going-away party for them, and my father would be sworn in to watch over the empty house. Proper attire for the men was whatever scraps of military uniform they still owned and could fit into.

When the family returned, they would find an old mannequin dressed in jeans, cowboy boots, plaid shirt, and cowboy hat, with an arrow stuck in its back, hanging in their yard. "The sheriff" would tell them the person had been found trespassing on their property, but he had taken care of it. This charade went on for several years.

LBJ

In 1964 Lyndon B. Johnson visited Dayton while campaigning for the presidency. A luncheon was held at Hawthorn Hill (Orville Wright's former home) for President Johnson and twenty-five other people, including my parents. Dad had known Johnson from his congressional years, and Johnson acted as though he remembered my father as well, even though he was in the Senate while my father was in the House. My mother was thrilled to be having lunch with President Johnson. Dad always admired Johnson because he believed that Johnson had inherited rather than created many of his problems, and was doing the best he could under the circumstances.

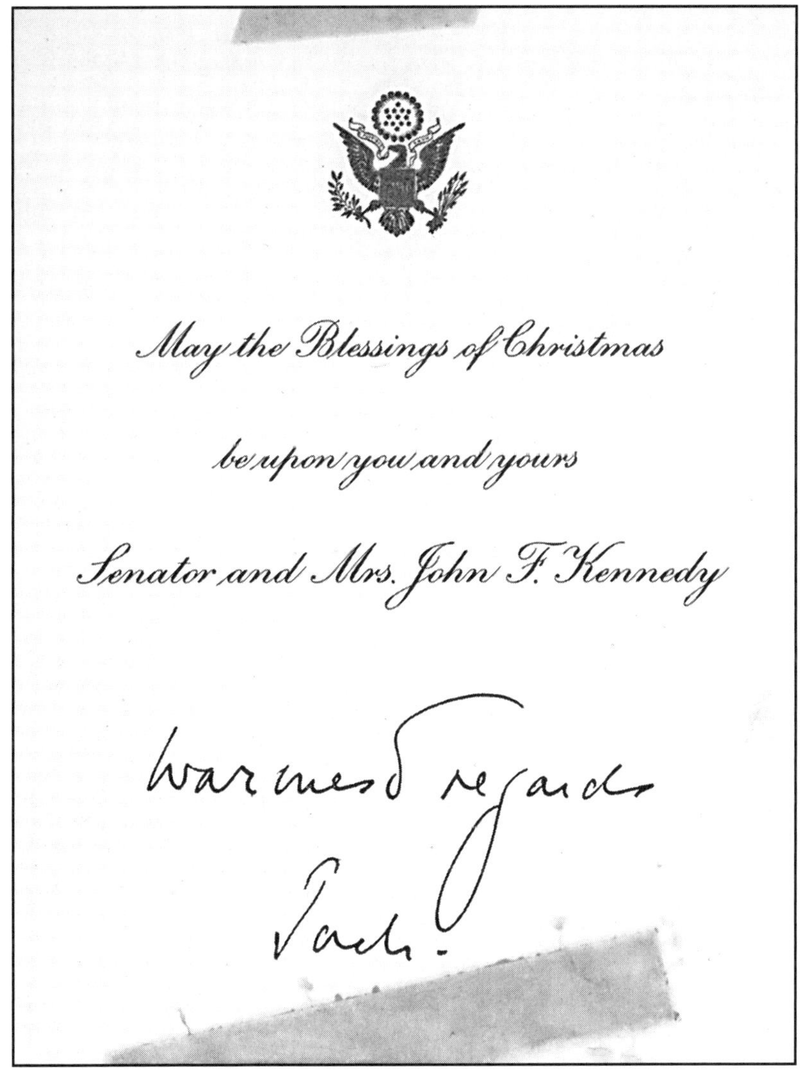

1959 Christmas card from John F. Kennedy to Eddie Breen.

The only thing I personally remember about the day was that President Johnson went to the Montgomery County Fairgrounds to give a speech. My brother and I had joined my parents, and we stood nearby. When Johnson finished, he reached to shake my hand. Afraid of this strange man, I held my hand back. I recall that Johnson made a joke of it and thought it was funny. Fortunately for me, President Johnson loved children and was always kind to them.

The Seer

One of our more unusual dinner guests was Jeanne Dixon, the astrologer and psychic. The Junior League had invited her to give a talk at their Town Hall Lecture Series, and my mother was asked to host a dinner party. At the party, Mrs. Dixon made a prediction for each of the guests. The dinner party turned out to be a big success and was talked about for years by everyone who had attended. Alee Turner, our family cook, told me that as Mrs. Dixon was leaving she went into the kitchen to thank Alee and her assistants for the wonderful vegetarian meal. Mrs. Dixon made her a prediction, and according to Alee, many years later, it came true. She was not the skeptic that my father was.

WINDING DOWN

Cindy Breen (on camel), Robert Breen (front), and Connie (reluctantly holding the beast's head) pose with a local tribesman on a visit to North Africa in 1971.

In 1967, my father left his consulting position with the county commission to manage Stillwater Hospital. In 1969, he retired completely. He spent the 1970s traveling, having lunch with friends, and more, but life was relatively quiet compared to his past adventures. It was during those retirement years, when I was in high school, that I heard most of his stories. Sometimes we would take family trips to Washington D.C., Italy, or North Africa and he would show us the sites that marked high points of his life. We walked the beach near Casablanca, where he had landed many years before with the Western Task Force. And we once spent a day in Naples, Italy, looking for the barone he once knew, only to find at the end of an exhaustive search that he had long since passed away. Dad also discovered that the large caves the barone had used to protect the frightened Italian citizens during German air raids were gone and nearly forgotten by the younger generation. The news distressed him.

One night in Munich, Germany, we were trying to find a cab to our hotel after a night at the opera. One eventually stopped, but the driver was very drunk. My father got into the front seat with him while the rest of the family piled into the back. The driver took off at a high speed and continued to drive very fast as my father spoke with him in German. Suddenly, the driver appeared very agitated and slammed on the brakes. He told us to get out and then sped off, leaving us stranded. My mother, of course, wanted to know what my father had said to the man and was more than a little exasperated at his reply. "I just asked him if he had been in the German army. He said that he'd been stationed in North Africa, so I told him that I had been in the American army and also stationed in North Africa. When I told him that I remembered marching a lot of blindfolded German prisoners to the docks in Algiers he got very angry. I guess he was one of them." Tiredly, we walked back to our hotel along the dark streets of Munich without another car in sight.

On trips to Washington, my father would take us to the offices of various congressmen or senators that he knew, and then to the congressional dining room for a meal. He would recall the more interesting events that had taken place during his time there, and then we would go onto the House floor and sit in the speaker's chair. He always explained to us the importance of that chair and told us stories of past speakers he knew.

In his retirement, my father liked to provide opportunities not only for his own children, but for others as well. He received many invitations to visit local elementary and high schools, and he tried to visit as many classrooms as he could. If a project involved children, he always made a special effort to be there.

Somehow both he and MaryLouise maintained friendships at high governmental levels and in both parties throughout their lives, which in turn provided us with many an eye-opening experience. Dad once sent a friend and me to Washington to participate in a week-long political forum held in the committee hearing rooms on Capitol Hill, then made

Thanks to his wealth of friendships, political and otherwise, that he maintained over the years, Eddie Breen was able to provide unusual experiences for his family and friends. Here, Terri Frick, the daughter of his niece, attended Ronald Reagan's second inaugural ball in January, 1985 along with the author.

arrangements for another friend, Mark Smith, and a Finnish exchange student living with us for the summer, to meet with the sergeant at arms of the United States House of Representatives. By chance, they also met his old friend, Senator Hubert Humphrey. In 1976, I wanted to go to New York City for the Democratic convention, but our local Democratic party leader said that one ticket for opening night was the best he could do. Dad called (by this time) former Vice President Hubert Humphrey who promptly gave him three tickets for all four nights with front

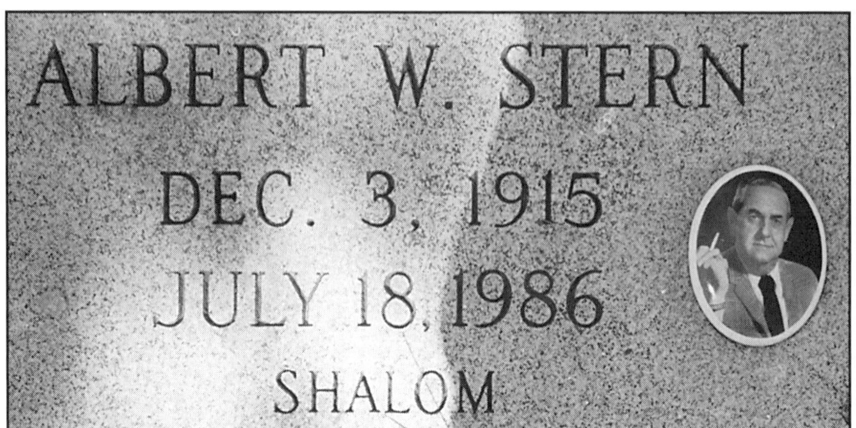

Albert Stern's tombstone, Mount Hope Cemetery, Champaign, Illinois.

row seats and passes to all the parties. He also arranged for my brother, a friend, and me to have a room down the hall from him and assured Dad that he would look after us while we were in New York.

After the 1984 election, Dad arranged front row seats for his brother's granddaughter, Terri Frick, and me to attend President Ronald Reagan's inauguration, as well as several parties and one of the inaugural balls. (He had made similar arrangements for my mother and me after the 1980 election; although a liberal Democrat when it came to civil and human rights, he was otherwise quite conservative and had many Republican friends. His popularity as a vote getter always crossed party lines.)

§

Albert Stern continued to be a presence in our lives, calling weekly and visiting Dayton often. (Never Maine, however. I suspect my aunt didn't approve of Albert.) By the mid-1980s, he was long retired and living in Florida. While my father could no longer visit him, I occasionally did, and the trips were always memorable, confirming the qualities that my father liked in him—a man full of fun who lived life large. His death in 1986 was a sad event for all of us, although we still laugh at the photo on his tombstone. The photo sat in his Florida home for several years before his death, and he told us repeatedly that it was intended for his tombstone. I guess we never quite believed him until we saw it.

§

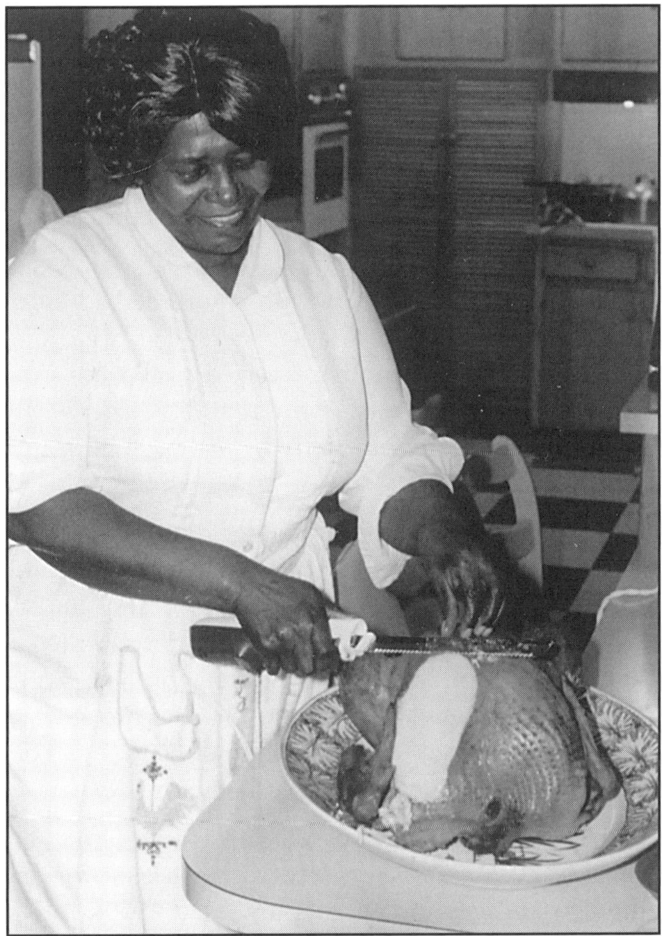

*Alee Turner started working for Eddie Breen as a
housekeeper at the Biltmore Hotel in the 1930s. Over thirty-
five years later, she still cooked for him when he had parties
at his home. He always maintained that he enjoyed talking
to Alee in the kitchen far more than he enjoyed the parties.*

By 1984, chronic diabetes and possibly the after-effects of wartime
mustard gas exposure caught up with my father; he was admitted to the
Dayton Veterans Hospital in accordance with his wishes. He had always
told us if he were ever to become incapacitated, he wanted to be placed
in the Veterans Hospital because he had so much respect for the army.
When he subsequently suffered a stroke and lost the ability to speak and
think clearly, he was transferred to a locked ward. Although he was able

to walk without any assistance, the hospital staff didn't want him to get lost due to mental confusion.

One morning, despite the security measures, my mother received a phone call from a frantic nurse telling her that Dad and two other men were missing. Another more experienced nurse reassured my mother. "Don't worry," she said, "they always go home. He'll probably turn up at your house in Kettering."

Several hours later, the two men with whom he had escaped were discovered at their homes, but my father was still at large. Another two hours passed, and finally my mother received a call from a man at the corner of Third and Main streets. Dad was at the corner where the old Phillips House Hotel used to be, where he had been born in 1908. He had gone home.

Beyond his immediate family, my father didn't speak often of his past life, and he never gossiped to outsiders about the famous people he knew (nor did MaryLouise, for that matter). At a dinner party, if pressed, he would tell one or two innocuous stories and then disappear into the kitchen to laugh and joke with the cooks and waiters. They would tell him to go out and enjoy the party, but he was always happiest in the kitchen area because it reminded him of his younger days in the hotel business.

Many of the people my father worked with as a young adult remained a part of his life, even years later. Alee Turner began working for my father at the Biltmore as a housekeeper in the late 1930s, and thirty-five years later she was still cooking at our home. She was a dear friend to both my mother and father, and she was my friend, too. During dinner parties, when my brother and I were supposed to be asleep, she would allow us to sneak into the kitchen and sample the party food before returning to bed.

As reticent as he was with friends and reporters about his experiences, my father always seemed to take special pleasure in talking to me. After he had retired, we would meet for lunch five days a week at a local restaurant, Neil's Heritage House, owned and operated by Walter Schaller who was something of a local legend in the hospitality industry. Carol Leatherman, the longtime hostess, seated us at the same table day in and day out, and I would listen to my father talk as the waitress brought his usual—a beef hotshot (a sandwich that's a Dayton

When Ed Breen became ill toward the end of his life, cartoonist Milton Caniff mentioned him in the comic strip Steve Canyon *out of respect for his childhood friend and fellow Boy Scout. Caniff passed away in 1988, three years before his friend. Courtesy of Harry Guyton and the Milton Caniff Collection,* The Ohio State University Cartoon Research Library.

speciality) and a glass of iced tea. His stories never bored me, and I'm grateful he shared them.

After lunch, Dad and I would go from booth to booth talking to his friends. The other retired men had the same routine as my father, always sitting in the same booth and eating the same food. He enjoyed this routine immensely, and so did I.

One thing that irritated him was when people approached and said, "Eddie, you sure did a great job 'mayoring' the city of Dayton." Or they might say to me, "When I first moved to Dayton, your father was 'mayoring' the city." Each time this occurred, I knew that my father would shortly say to me—as soon as the person had left—"You don't 'mayor' a city, you 'govern' a city." When Dad became ill for the last time and was living permanently at the Veterans Hospital, some of the older male nurses would make reference to when he 'mayored' the city. When he failed to make his usual correction, I realized for the first time that he was truly ill and would not be getting better.

In 1983, my mother and her good friends threw a surprise party for my father's seventy-fifth birthday. It was held at the home of Weezie McGinnis, one block from the home my father and his brother and sister bought for his parents. My father was completely surprised and a little embarrassed by all the attention, but was very happy to see all his friends together, especially the bartenders he had known from his hotel days. He was surprised to receive a well-preserved bottle of liquor from the Phillips House Bar, and commented that the fact that the liquor was still in the bottle was a bigger feat than him turning seventy-five.

One of the biggest events in the last years of Dad's life was my marriage in 1987. My wedding was in the latter part of January on the coldest day of the year. Dad was in a wheelchair and had lost most of his ability to talk. Two of the kind nurses at the Veterans Hospital bundled him up, put him into a large ambulance, and rode to the church with him. They placed him in the front row next to my mother. It meant a great deal for him to be there and he greeted many of the guests with a firm handshake.

My father's childhood friend, Milton Caniff, the famous cartoonist, was nearing the end of his life, too. Milton lived far away from Ohio, but had received word that my father was very ill. Several days later, my father's name was used in Milton's comic strip, *Steve Canyon*. It was Milton's way of saying "get well" to his old friend. The nurses at the Veterans Hospital had the comic strip enlarged and hung on the wall above Dad's bed. Another man, who remembered my father from his childhood, was surprised to see the name "Ed Breen" in his local Alaskan paper's comics. He flew to Dayton the following week to visit my father and told us that as a young boy growing up in a Dayton orphanage, he had come to know my father. Although the man had badly wanted to drop out of school, Dad promised that if he graduated, he would introduce him to the famous pilots he knew such as Carl Cover, the chief test pilot for Douglas aircraft. When the boy graduated, my father kept his promise, and the man eventually became a test pilot himself.

§

Edward G. Breen, died in May 1991. My sister, brother and mother spent time with him the day he died. I was able to be with him the day before. He had made a few requests beforehand in keeping with his simple lifestyle. He asked to be buried in a blue terry cloth bathrobe, the heavy, thick sort he used to wear after his early morning swims in

Maine. He wanted warm, white wool socks on his feet. He didn't want his feet to get cold, as he would often joke. He also requested that he be buried in a standard, wooden, military-issued coffin, the kind that had been used to bury his comrades in arms in World War II. Finally, he wanted a lone bugler to play taps. It was a tune that he had become all too familiar with while overseas, and he knew the words to that haunting ballad by heart.

I never knew my father to be afraid of anything, including death. Death, he used to say, was like boarding a train traveling over the horizon, and getting off on the other side.

On June 27, 1991, Ambassador Tony P. Hall, then the congressman representing Dad's former district, concluded his tribute on the floor of the United States House of Representatives with these words:

> *During his years in government service, Mr. Breen established himself as a true leader. One of his great strengths was his ability to pull together diverse factions. He was always dignified, yet he could reach out to everyone. He was an inspiration to the young leaders of Dayton.*
>
> *Mr. Breen set the highest standards for community service. As the Representative who holds the seat he once occupied, I am reminded of his record of service which can serve as a model for the leaders of today and tomorrow.*

§

In 2003, a memorial stone honoring Edward G. Breen was added to Dayton, Ohio's Walk of Fame. It reads:

Edward Grimes Breen

1908–1991

U. S. Representative, Mayor of Dayton

County Commissioner

Political activist for the common man

who worked diligently for a better community.

He supported education, parks and recreation and

a better quality of life for Miami Valley residents.

Like many, the Breen family history is a story filled with comedy, drama, and sadness. I have to thank my father, my grandfather, and all the generations of Breen storytellers for continuing the tradition of telling a good tale. I hope my children will continue to share these stories when they grow up and have children of their own. They may not be able to resist—it's in their blood. That old Irish baloney never goes stale.

It is also worth noting that the "players" in this book were intensely discreet people who would never have revealed these stories outside of immediate family during their lifetimes. My father had numerous friendships dating back to those forged in the Phillips House and Biltmore dining rooms, as did my aunt, MaryLouise. To outsiders, she was a master of interesting, clever conversation that utterly excluded gossip about the important people she knew. My father's trick was to remain busy—the person asking a few too many questions about a famous friend would find Eddie politely excusing himself in the midst of a party to dash into the kitchen claiming his help was needed with the drinks or appetizers.

Telling these stories now, as I said in the introduction, was an opportunity to glimpse a bygone era, see examples of lives well-lived, and, perhaps, in viewing one family's trajectory, to learn a little bit more about the breadth of the American experience. My family and I have benefitted as well, coming to understand and admire these people even more than we had in the past.

While my father and MaryLouise, especially, would have been uncomfortable with this public airing, I know that at least my father would have understood the importance of sharing "history in the making" with another generation. I hope that some of you will be intrigued enough to learn more about events from the not-so-distant past and the men and women who participated in them. History isn't just great men fighting great wars, nor is it just great political leaders, it is also the people around you and their stories; knowing those stories can change how we live and think.

We are remembered in life for the good or the bad we did while walking this earth. So it is with this hope that I leave you: if you are an adult, take time to have a meaningful talk with a child. If you are a child, ask your parents or grandparents to tell you the stories of their own lives. The very best thing we can do for each other in this world is to share and care. It doesn't take money—it takes a heart.

Best wishes to all,
Edward Focke Breen

ACKNOWLEDGMENTS

Iwould like to thank my father-in-law James M. Taylor and my friend
and fellow teacher, Liz Whipps; without their interest and strong
encouragement to "write it all down" this book would never have seen
the light of day.

I wish to thank my publishers, Harold Maguire and Cheryl Towers,
at The Local History Company for having faith in the book. This has
been a new experience for me and I could not have gotten through it
without their patience and advice on this project. Their support was
greatly appreciated. I would also like to thank editor Christine Cooper,
archivist Mandy Fields, proofreader Noreen Greeno, and interns Megan
Boyd and Emily DeVore, who all helped me make sense of mountains
of material.

Tribute is due to the memories of the late Ohio Governor James M.
Cox, the late Clarence J. McLin Sr. and the late Miriam Rosenthal; without the love and support of these key people, my father never would
have had a career in politics. They, as well as many hundreds of other
people, made it possible.

I would also like to remember the late Albert Stern of Champaign,
Illinois and Longboat Key, Florida and the late Donald Ruhlman, Sr.
of Dayton, Ohio. They witnessed the best and worst of times with my
father. My family is forever grateful that we had a chance to know them
both.

My family also wishes to acknowledge the following: the late Al Horstman former chairman of the Montgomery County Democratic Party
and a close personal friend of my father's; Richard Cull Jr. who, as a
reporter, covered my father both in Dayton and later on in Washington,
D.C.; Laurence Newman, a journalist and editor who came to know our
family as a friend; Dale Huffman, a reporter and columnist who was the
last to interview my father and mother together and was responsible for
the last formal picture of our family together, a picture we will cherish
for a lifetime; the late Andy Drysdale, Dad's marvelous press secretary;
Don Timmons, a reporter who covered my father during his county

commission years; journalists Robert Daley, who covered my father's career for the Dayton *Journal-Herald*, and Maxwell Nathan along with the late Si Burick of the *Dayton Daily News*; the late Marj Heyduck, an editor and columnist whose humor and bright outlook on life as well as her many colorful hats will never be forgotten; and the late W. Sumpter McIntosh, businessman and civil rights leader, whose friendship my father always held in high esteem.

I am forever grateful to my cousin, John G. Breen, who as a young man witnessed many of these events, and who was invaluable to me as a reference source.

Special thanks to the wonderful staff in the Special Collections and Archives Division of the Paul Laurence Dunbar Library at Wright State University, Dayton, Ohio, especially archivist Toni Jeske, who was invaluable to me in locating photographs and old letters. Likewise, Elli Bambakidis, the archival reference librarian at the Dayton Metro Library, has repeatedly proven herself to be an invaluable resource. In addition, the staff at the *Dayton Daily News* research library provided generous help and assistance, especially Martha Hild and Phillip Elam who located wonderful old photos. I am also indebted to archivist MaryRose Grossman of the Research Department of The John F. Kennedy Presidential Library in Boston, as well as P.J. Santos of the Miss America Organization, Atlantic City, N.J.

I would like to acknowledge the following persons for a lifetime of friendship: Robert and Susan Breen, and their children, Isabelle and Beckman; and Craig and Missy Murakami. Thanks also to Bob Williams, Gregg Daubert, Mark P. Smith, Nancy T. Gauger, Therese S. Gordan, Lucy Bell Jarka-Sellers, Quintin Lindsmith, the late Lupe Coleman, and the late Alee Turner.

I also wish to thank the following people who have supported me over the years: Jan Breen, Cindy W. Breen, Thomas M. Ott, Jean Powell, Roger J. Makley, Robert E. Ruhlman, James J. Mischler Jr., Carolyn Robinson, Wayne and Betty Rogge Morse, Don Dahlman, Father Bertram Buby, Father James Manning, Father Joseph Goetz, Father Johann Roten, Father James Gower, Sister Jean Frisk, Jeanne Kelly, Marilyn Taylor, Anne Ferneding, Johanna Hill, Milly Hubler, Lori Dierken, Patrick W. Dugan, Grayce Ward, Curt Dalton, Peirce Woodward, Leslie Tekamp, Chuck Hamlin, William J. Focke, Polly Tonini, Gretchen Focke, David B. Brown, the late Adelaide B. Frick, William K. Cochrane, the late Betty

H. Frecker, J. Andrew Leakas, James C. Deuser, William Pflaum, Betsy Moore, Meryl Spurlin, Richard Ross, and Sally McBride Solarek.

Finally, I would like to remember the late Richard (Dick) Netzorg of Chicago, Illinois, a member of the famed 10th Mountain Ski Division during World War II; he was a very brave man who did his best, and a man of many talents who was much loved by our family.

Edward Focke Breen

BREEN AND BECKMAN FAMILY GENEALOGY

The lineage of the family members featured most prominently within the book are in bold type. Offspring of other family members are not listed. Numbers prior to a name indicate the generation to which they belong.

THE BREEN FAMILY

1 Daniel Breen, Sr. (b. Kilbrean More, Ireland, 1790, d. unknown), m. **Mary Hayes** (b. Kilbrean More, Ireland. 1794, d. unknown), 1809

Daniel and Mary's children (all born Kilbrean More, Ireland):

2 John (b. 1814-death date unknown)

2 Patrick (b. 1824, d. Xenia, OH, 1900), m. Catherine Walsh, 1863, Xenia, OH

2 Catherine (b. 1831, d. Xenia, OH, 1920), m. William Edgeworth (1825-1895), Xenia, OH, 1852

2 Daniel, Jr. (b. 1825, d. Xenia, OH, 1890), m. Catherine Sullivan, 1859

2 Maurice Breen (b. 1828, d. Marion, Ohio, 1906), m. Elizabeth Fitzgerald, Killarney, January, 1851 (she passed away; he emigrated), m. **Mary O'Neal**, November, 1851 (b. Fermoy, Ireland, 1833, d. Xenia, OH, 1872)

Maurice and Mary's children (all born Xenia, Ohio):

3 Mary (1852-death date unknown)

3 Catherine (1854-1892)

3 Daniel (1856-1876)

3 John P. Breen (b. 1860, d. Dayton, 1936), m. **Katherine Beckman**, 1896 (see Beckman family information following)

John P. and Katherine's children (all born Dayton, Ohio):

4 Henry Morse Breen (b. 1898, died Cleveland, 1899)

4 John Beckman Breen (1900-1974), m. Adelaide Gilbert (1907-1946), Catherine Skinner Scully (1910-1985)

John & Adelaide's children (b. Dayton, OH):

5 John Gilbert (1932-), m. Janice Loftus, 1955

5 Adelaide Beckman (Becky) (1938-1992), m. Robert Frick, 1962

4 MaryLouise Breen Garrity (b. 1904, d. 2000), m. Robert Garrity (1906-1995), 1947. No children.

4 Edward Grimes Breen (1908-1991), m. **Constance Focke** (1928-), 1956

Eddie and Connie's children (all born Dayton, Ohio):

5 Edward Focke Breen (1957-), m. Catherine Taylor, 1987

5 Robert Beckman Breen (1958-), m. Susan Livingston, 1997

5 Cynthia Ward Breen (1962-), a. 1967

3 Maurice, Jr. (1863, d. Marion, OH, 1905)

3 Hanna (b. 1864, died as a child, date unknown)

3 Michael (b. 1866, d. Dayton, OH, 1946)

3 Frank (b. 1870, died near New York City in the 1930s)

The Beckman Family

1 Herman Beckman (b. Germany, 1802, died Cleveland, Ohio, 1886), m. **Anna Maria Elizabeth Heidacker** (b. Germany, 1811, died Germany, 1862), 1830

Herman Beckman's children (17 children, all born Wallenhorst, Germany)

2 Herman, Jr. (1822-1899, died Cleveland, Ohio)

2 Henry Beckman (1832-1887, died Cleveland, Ohio), m. **Louisa Erhard** (b. Bethlehem, PA, 1835, d. Cleveland, Ohio, 1899), 1854

Henry and Louisa's children (all born Cleveland, Ohio):

3 Louise (1855-1937), m. Fred Shale

3 Henry, Jr. (1856-1888), m. Ann Holland, 1886

3 Teresa (1861-1890), m. Henry Ostendorf, 1887

3 Anna (1863-1937), m. John Ohmer, 1886

3 Josephine (1867-1934), m. John Callaghan, 1886

3 Francis H. (1869-1869)

3 Katherine (1870, died Dayton, 1953), m. **John P. Breen**, 1896 (see children under John P. Breen entry)

3 Henrietta (1875-1949), m. Henry John Edwards (1872-1954), 1897

BIBLIOGRAPHY

PUBLISHED MATERIAL

Atkins, Rick, *An Army at Dawn: The War in Africa, 1942-1943 (Volume One, The Liberation Trilogy)*. Henry Holt and Company, New York, 2002.

————, *The Day of Battle: The War in Sicily and Italy, 1943-1944 (Volume Two, The Liberation Trilogy)*. Henry Holt and Company, New York, 2007.

Batz, Bob, "Niece of Orville's housekeeper recalls fun visits to Hawthorn Hill," *Dayton Daily News*, Sunday, July 13, 2003.

Bliven, Bruce, Jr., *The Story of D-DAY June 6, 1944*, 50th Anniversary Edition. Random House, New York, 1956.

Butler, Susan, *East To The Dawn: The Life Of Amelia Earhart*. Addison-Wesley, Reading MA 1997.

Cordery, Stacy A., *Alice: Alice Roosevelt Longworth from White House Princess to Washington Power Broker*. Viking Penguin, New York, 2007.

Dalton, Curt, *Through Flood, Through Fire: Personal Stories from Survivors of the Dayton Flood of 1913*. Mazer Co., 2001.

DeBrosse, Jim, "Dillinger's Gun: How the infamous fugitive was captured in Dayton," *Dayton Daily News*, June 6, 2004.

Dwiggins, Don, Forward by Lowell Thomas, *Hollywood Pilot: The Biography of Paul Mantz*. Doubleday & Company, Inc., Garden City, New York, 1967.

Eckert, Allan W., *A Time of Terror: The Great Dayton Flood*. Little, Brown & Company (Canada) Limited, 1965.

Felsenthal, Carol, Alice Roosevelt Longworth. G.P. Putnam's Sons, New York, 1988.

Girardin, G. Russell with Helmer, William J., Dillinger: *The Untold Story*. Indiana University Press, Bloomington, and Indianapolis, Indiana, 1994.

Goerner, Fred, *The Search for Amelia Earhart, The full story of a struggle begun in 1960 to unlock the secrets of a fantastic 30-year-old mystery.* Doubleday & Company Inc., Garden City, New York, 1966.

Hamilton, Charles V., *The Political Biography of an American Dilemma*. Athenum, New York, 1991.

Hanson, Erica, *A Cultural History of the United States through the Decades: The 1920s*. Lucent Books Inc., San Diego, California, 1999.

Hauff, Warren R. (writer and collector), History Committee, Miami Valley Council Boy Scouts of America (editor), Caniff, Milton (illustrator), *Fun and Service; A history of the Boy Scouts of America in the Miami Valley Council*. Miami Valley Council Boy Scouts of America, Dayton, Ohio, 1970.

Helfrich, G.W. and O'Neil, Gladys, *Lost Bar Harbor*. Down East Books Camden, Maine, 1982.

The Lincoln Herald, The Commemorative Issue, 1897-1997, Spring 1997. Lincoln Memorial University Press, Harrogate, Tennessee.

Lord, Walter, *A Night To Remember*. Henry Holt and Company, New York, 1955.

Matera, Dary, *John Dillinger: The Life & Times of America's First Celebrity Criminal*. Carroll & Graf Publishers, 2004.

McCullough, David, *Truman*. Simon & Schuster, New York, London, 1992.

Miller, William "Fishbait", as told to Frances Spatz Leighton, *Fishbait: The Memoirs of the Congressional Doorkeeper*. Prentice-Hall,Inc., Englewood Cliffs, N.J. 1977.

Montgomery County, Ohio History, 1989 (A history written by the people of Montgomery County, Ohio and compiled and published by the Montgomery History Planning Committee). Printed by Taylor Publishing Co., Dallas, Texas, 1990.

Morison, Samuel Eliot. *History of United States Naval Operations in World War II: Vol. IX Sicily, Salerno, Anzio*. January 1943-June 1944. Boston: Little, Brown, and Co., 1954.

Ostendorf, Lloyd, *Mr. Lincoln Came To Dayton: A Centennial Account of Abraham Lincoln's Visit To Dayton, Ohio 1859.* The Otterbein Press Dayton, Ohio 1959.

Powell, Adam Clayton Powell Jr., Foreword by Adam Clayton Powell III, *Adam: The Autobiography of Adam Clayton Powell Jr.* Kensington Publishing Corp. New York, 1971.

Powell, Adam Clayton Jr., *Letter to Mr. Morris H. Simmons.* President LOCAL NAACP, 1950

Press, Petra, *A Cultural History of the United States through the Decades: The 1930s.* Lucent Books Inc., San Diego, California, 1999.

Roosevelt, Elliott, *Eleanor Roosevelt with Love/A Centenary Remembrance.* Lodestar Books, E. P. Dutton, New York, 1984.

Sandoval-Strausz, A.K., *Hotel/An American History.* Yale University Press, New Haven and London, 2007.

Zumwald, Teresa (text), Christian, Marvin (photo research), Rollins, Ron (editing), *For the Love of Dayton: Life in the Miami Valley 1796 –1996.* Designed and produced by Sol Smith, BFS Printing, for the *Dayton Daily News*, Dayton, Ohio, 1996.

Unpublished material, interviews, & Miscellaneous

Johannes Beckmann of Wallenhorst, Germany who provided photos of his father, Johannes Beckmann, Sr., as well as letters and other documentation from the time period 1940-1945.

Joe Focke who united the Breen and Beckmann families from America and Germany after a seventy year separation that resulted in letters and photos of Beckmann relatives being sent to America, and for his translation of the materials.

Life inside the Phillips House Hotel during and after the 1913 flood, taken from unpublished notes written by **MaryLouise Breen Garrity**.

Stories regarding the childhood of Constance Focke told to the author by **Jack and Phyliss Heck** (former *Dayton Daily News* columnist) and **Ginny Whalen.**

Stories on the life of MaryLouise Breen Garrity covering the period 1935-1945, and stories regarding the wedding of Edward G. Breen to Constance Focke told to the author by **John Ohmer Hubler.** He witnessed many of these stories in Madrid, Spain during the war years, and later as best man and confidant to Edward G. Breen.

Ohmer family tree and other related material provided by **Milly Hubler**.

Stories of "The Spot" train depot restaurant in Huntington, Indiana and other such places that have since vanished from the American landscape told to the author by **Jeanne Kelly** who grew up in Huntington and knew "The Spot" first-hand.

Photos and stories on the life of James M. Cox told to the author by **Polly Evans Tonini**, who lived in the Cox home as a child.

Life in North Africa and Italy during World War II, taken from some of the many war stories told to the author by **Lieutenant Albert Stern** at his retirement home in Long Boat Key, Florida, during the spring of 1976.

Edward Breen with President Truman in Cincinnati on campaign train October 11, 1948. Truman Library, http://www.trumanlibrary.org/publicpapers/index.php?pid=1981&st=&st1=Public Papers, **Truman Presidential Museum & Library**.

Photo by Robert Breen.

Edward Focke Breen

The author is an Ohio native and school teacher who has spent a lifetime traveling in Europe, North Africa, and the Americas. A graduate of Capital University who has done post-graduate work at Antioch University, he is married to Catherine Taylor, a writer and former magazine editor. They and their two sons live in the Dayton area and spend summers at their home in coastal Maine.

The author's immediate family members (Edward G. (Eddie) Breen, Constance Focke Breen, MaryLouise Breen Garrity, John P. Breen, and Katherine Beckman Breen) are deeply imbedded throughout the story and are therefore not indexed separately except where they appear in images or their captions. Page references in italic indicate photographs, illustrations, or images of historical documents.